Brilliant guides

What you need to know and how to do it

When you're working on your computer and come up against a problem that you're unsure how to solve or want to accomplish something in an application that you aren't sure how to do, where do you look? Manuals and traditional training guides are usually too big and unwieldy and are intended to be used as end-to-end training resources, making it hard to get to the info you need right away without having to wade through pages of background information that you just don't need at that moment – and helplines are rarely that helpful!

Brilliant guides have been developed to allow you to find the info you need easily and without fuss and guide you through the task using a highly visual, step-by-step approach – providing exactly what you need to know when you need it!

Brilliant guides provide the quick, easy-to-access information that you need, using a table of contents and troubleshooting guide to help you find exactly what you need to know, and then presenting each task in a visual manner. Numbered steps guide you through each task or problem, using numerous screenshots to illustrate each step. Added features include 'See also . . .' boxes that point you to related tasks and information in the book, while 'Did you know?' sections alert you to relevant expert tips, tricks and advice to further expand your skills and knowledge.

In addition to covering all major office PC applications, and related computing subjects, the *Brilliant* series also contains titles that will help you in every aspect of your working life, such as writing the perfect CV, answering the toughest interview questions and moving on in your career.

Brilliant guides are the light at the end of the tunnel when you are faced with any minor or major task.

Author's dedication and acknowledgements

This book is for N. She makes it all possible without even knowing it.

No book is ever written in a vacuum, so I would like to thank Alisa Miller, for her generosity in allowing me to use her website to illustrate many of the points, Nike, for telling me when enough was enough and I had to come away from my laptop screen and Neil Salkind for never taking no for an answer and persevering with me.

About the author

David Amerland has been actively involved in Web and search technologies and practices since 1995, when the Internet became a viable means of online commerce. A former journalist, he has worked in the retail and business communication sectors for, among others, the John Lewis Partnership. He has transferred his experience of what works offline, when helping to create brands and visibility, into his work online. Currently, he is involved in guiding international companies in how to succeed online across cultural divides and outside their home territory borders. When he is not working, he unwinds by surfing and catching up with the latest breakthroughs in quantum mechanics and particle physics.

Acknowledgements

We are grateful to the following for permission to reproduce copyright material:

Screenshots from Alisa Miller's website courtesy of Alisa Miller; Facebook screenshots courtesy of Facebook, Inc.; Englishinabox and Burlington English screenshots from www. Englishinabox.com, with thanks to English In a Box, the web's most powerful, interactive, language learning method; AuditMyPC screenshots courtesy of AuditMyPC.com; John Lewis homepage courtesy of John Lewis; Axemedia screenshot courtesy of Axemedia; StumbleUpon screenshot courtesy of StumbleUpon.com; Delicious Home/Fresh Bookmarks screenshot reproduced with permission of Yahoo! Inc. © 2010 Yahoo! Inc. YAHOO!, the YAHOO! logo and DELICIOUS and the DELICIOUS logo are registered trademarks of Yahoo! Inc.; Yahoo! screenshot courtesy of Yahoo! Inc.; Copyscape screenshot courtesy of Indigo Stream Technologies; Tumblr.com screenshots courtesy of Tumblr Inc.

In some instances we have been unable to trace the owners of copyright material, and we would appreciate any information that would enable us to do so.

Contents

Introduction

Welcome to *Brilliant Search Engine Optimisation*. 'SEO' is one of the most cryptic acronyms on the Web. Depending on who you talk to about it you will get different accounts of what it is and how it should be done. Programmers think that it has to do with site layout and search engine algorithms. Web designers will talk about JavaScript and the use of text links on your website. Online marketers will talk about social networking and online viral campaigns and publicists will tell you that it is all about search engine marketing (popularly known as SEM) and online news campaigns.

The multitude of voices arguing over what SEO really is usually drown out those of the search engine optimisers themselves, who are only concerned with what it does: it makes your website visible to as many people as possible.

Brilliant Search Engine Optimisation is exactly about the final description above. I assume that you are interested in SEO because you either have a website you want to optimise or you are involved in some project where search engine optimisation is a requirement. Either way, you have little time to waste on theory, which simply fills pages, so everything detailed here is practical.

Find what you need to know – when you need it

This book consists of ten chapters. Each of these chapters covers an aspect of vital SEO knowledge that you will need in order to ensure your website is ranked high on the search engine results pages of Google, Yahoo! and Bing. The truth about SEO, which few people realise, is that it is strictly logical. Everything you see on the Web and everything search engines do depends on mathematics.

How you'll learn

Find what you need to know – when you need it

Jargon busters

Troubleshooting guide

Spelling

This means that it can be learnt, understood and then worked on so you achieve the desired result. It gets better than this. To gain the results you need in SEO, you do not need to be a maths wizard. The truth is, you do not even need to be an SEO expert. All you need to do is understand *why* something happens, then apply the cause-and-effect result so that your website benefits.

It really is that simple. I hope, throughout the book, you will find the instructions I have given easy to follow and rewarding. The Web really is the great equaliser when it comes to creating wealth. To make it work for you, you need a good idea, some knowledge and the rest is hard work.

Hopefully the knowledge you will find in this book is just what you need to help you get to the next level.

Jargon busters

Key terms are explained in the 'Jargon buster' feature as you work through the chapters. As an easy-to-find reference, key terms also appear at the end of the book.

Troubleshooting guide

This book offers quick and easy ways to diagnose and solve common problems that you might encounter, using the Troubleshooting guide. The problems are grouped into categories that are presented alphabetically.

Spelling

We have used UK spelling conventions throughout this book. You may therefore notice some inconsistencies between the text and the software on your computer which is likely to have been developed in the US. We have, however, adopted US spelling for the words 'disk' and 'program' as these are commonly accepted throughout the world.

Instant SEO

Introduction

What is SEO? This question seems the most sensible place to start a book that has SEO as its subject. Search engine optimisation (SEO) is the term used for the set of practices webmasters engage in, in order to promote their websites to search engines.

The whole point of search engine optimisation is to make your website more visible to those who are most likely to need your products or services. In this regard, it has a lot to do with marketing and, as a matter of fact, as we shall see later on in the book, there is a convergence between the approach used to market your website online and optimise it so that it can be easily found.

In this chapter, you will explore some of the elements of SEO to discover which of them you can control (so should focus on) and which you can't (so should not really be worried about).

For instance, you will never be able to control what happens with search engines, what happens on the Web or what SEO activities your competitors engage in. What is of interest to us here is the elements that you *can* control.

You will also learn how you can start to optimise your website almost immediately.

What you'll do

Write keywords that help your SEO

Use Google AdWords

Create a Google AdWords account

Use alt and title attributes

Ensure your alt tags will be indexed by Google

Learn how to write alt tags

Learn what Black Hat SEO is (and how do you avoid it)

Writing keywords that help your SEO

▶

Keywords are one of the elements you can control absolutely and they deliver instant SEO success to you by beginning to work the moment you put them into play. The struggle every webmaster faces when optimising a website is that of writing keywords in the text, naturally, in a way that really helps the website in the organic search engine page results, which, these days, really only have any meaning when we discuss Google.

The ideal time to start optimising your website is before it is even designed by paying attention to some very specific design characteristics and discussing them with your web designer or web studio at the creation stage. The design of your website will play a significant role in the level of search engine-friendliness it displays. Even if your website has been designed and you have made some basic SEO mistakes, it may not be too late to rectify them now.

So, what can you do when you need to turn your website into a Google magnet and attract targeted visitors from relevant searches? Well, it is pretty simple.

■ **Think theme** If you're going to use keywords, think of the theme of your site and write all the keywords associated with that theme. Put each of the keywords you come up with under the headings 'Targeted' or 'General'. So, if your site is about estate agents in Wilmslow, Cheshire, then the search term 'estate agents' is a general term and the terms 'Cheshire estate agents' and 'Wilmslow estate agents' are targeted.

■ **Think bold** Unfortunately, what Google likes best in terms of keywords will make your site look like a seven-year-old's doodle, so the challenge is to find a way to stress the importance of the keywords without suddenly putting them in 20-point capital letters and underlining them. You can, however, make them bold (as long as you don't overdo it) and capitalise the odd one, provided it does not break up your site's design.

■ **Check density** Keyword density is an important element of optimisation for your website. Aim for between 1 and 3 per cent and use at least two more supportive keywords in a lower (0.5 to 2 per cent) density. If you are not sure about the keywords, then visit **http://articleannouncer.com/ tools/keyword.html**. Copy and paste your text and type in your target keywords. You can also actually work on it online, modifying it until the density is exactly right.

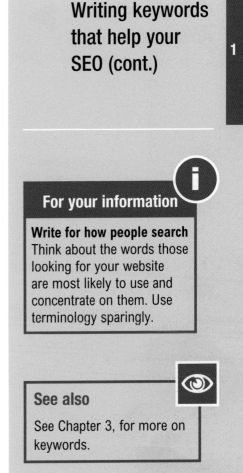

Make sure you don't overdo it. Keyword density works best when it is within what search engine algorithms consider to be the acceptable density of 'natural' writing. This means that your target keywords should not really rise about the 5% mark.

In order to achieve this after you have copied and pasted the article body, you will need to adjust the density of the keywords by either, using synonyms and reducing their occurrence or writing extra copy and increasing the overall number of words of the article.

Using Google AdWords

▶

Find out what the most popular keyword searches for your type of business are by putting the term in Google AdWords Google's online research tool (at: **https://adwords.google.com/select/KeywordToolExternal**).

1. Enter your main keyword in **Word or phrase** and your website name in **Website**. You can type more than one keyword, and a phrase, even, provided you use a separate line for each one.

2. Tick the box. Only show ideas containing my search terms. This will help you to narrow down the field and increase the relevancy of any keywords.

3. You can restrict your keyword search to your local geographic area.

4. If you want to get the full benefits of the keyword research Google gives you, you will need to create a Google Adwords account and login.

Jargon buster

Google AdWords – Pay Per Click contextual advertisement program, very common method of basic website advertisement.

Set Up Account

Which best describes you?

○ I have an email address and password I already use with Google services like AdSense, Gmail, Orkut, or the personal page.

◉ I do not use these other services.

Create a new Google Account for use with AdWords.
Make sure your email address is correct. You must receive email there in order to verify this account.

Email: [   ]
                          e.g. myname@example.com. This will be your username and sign-in.

Password: [   ]
                          Minimum of 6 characters in length. [?]

Re-enter password: [   ]

Type the characters you see in the picture below.

yqpini

[   ] &
Letters are not case-sensitive
By submitting this form, you agree to the Terms of Service & Privacy Policy

2 —— [Create Account »]

4

What is the most you would like to spend, on average, per day?

The daily budget [?] controls your costs. When the daily limit is reached, on average, your ad will stop showing for that day. (The budget controls the frequency of your ad.) Raise or lower your budget as often as you like.

Enter your daily budget: $ [   ]

What is the maximum you are willing to pay each time someone clicks on your ad?

You influence your ad's position by setting its maximum cost per click (CPC) [?]. The max CPC is the highest price you're willing to pay each time a user clicks on your ad. CPC can be changed as often as you like.

Enter your maximum CPC: $ [   ] (Minimum $0.01)
Higher CPCs lead to higher ad positions, which usually get more clicks.

Want to purchase the most clicks possible? To put your ad near the top position for all possible impressions, we estimate a budget of $40.00 and a max CPC of $1.3
▸ View Traffic Estimator - Enter a CPC and see the estimated rank, traffic, and costs for your keyword(s).

Three things to remember:

- Your ads won't start running until you activate your account by responding to an email we'll send you. You can always change your CPC and budget, or pause your account entirely.
- Your budget controls your spending. If your daily budget is $5.00 and there are 30 days in a month, you'll never be charged more than $150 in that month.
- Lower your costs by choosing more specific keywords, like red roses instead of flowers. Specific keywords are more likely to turn a click into a customer. Edit your keywords

Target customers by country or territory

Highlight the countries or territories on the left where you'd like your ad to appear, then click 'Add.' Select as many as you like. Your ads will appear in each location you select.

Available Countries and Territories   Selected Countries and/or Territories
┌─────────────────────────┐   ┌─────────────────────────┐
│ Finland   ▲ │   │   │
│ France   │   │   │
│ Germany   │   [Add »]   │   │
│ Hong Kong   │   │   │
│ Italy   │ [« Remove] │   │
│ Japan   │   │   │
│ Netherlands   │   │   │
│ Norway   │   │   │
│ Portugal   │   │   │
│ Singapore   ▼ │   │   │
└─────────────────────────┘   └─────────────────────────┘

5

1 Go to the Google AdWords home page (**www.adwords. google.com**) and click **Start now**.

2 Fill in your details and click **Create Account**.

3 Select the language in which you want your ads to display, choosing the language your customers are most likely to use.

4 Set up your ad budget by deciding on how much you want to spend per day.

5 Decide how targeted you want your ads to be. If you are selling worldwide you'll likely want to choose all countries and territories. If you are a physical business that ships throughout your country, choose your country only. If you are a local business that only sells locally, choose the customised option and your ads will only show up for customers within the geographical area you specify. Click **Continue** when you've made your choices.

Using alt and title attributes ▶

The days when an all-text site was considered sexy belong firmly in the last century. Today's sites need to catch and hold the visitor's eye in order for the content to work on them … and that means pictures. The problem is that pictures are invisible to search engines, so what works on human visitors does not work on the means you are trying to use to attract them there.

To create effective page content that will appeal to both human visitors and search engine spiders, you need to get the most out of every page element. One way to do this is to use alt and title attributes wherever you can. They increase your site's usability level and promotion possibilities if you clearly understand where to put them, when to use them and why.

The alt attribute is designed to be an alternative text description for images. Alt text displays before the image is loaded (if it's loaded at all) in the major browsers and instead of the image in text-based browsers such as Lynx. Alt is a required element for images and can only be used for image tags because its specific purpose is to describe images.

1 If you are using a content management system (CMS) to put content on your site, the Alternative Text (alt tag) data entry box allows you to describe an image accurately so that Google can understand what it is and index the content accurately. Depending on the CMS you use, the appropriate image description field will also sometimes be called 'Image description' or 'Image title'.

'Title Attribute' is a more generic field name used not just in picture descriptions, these days, but also in the description of links, tables, table rows and just about most things which need to be described to a search engine so that it can then 'see' them and understand what they are. They're more versatile than the alt attribute and many search engines' ranking algorithms read the text in title attributes as normal page content.

ⓘ For your information

Let's dispel one myth: there are rumours that alt tags do not matter and search engines discount them. This was temporarily true between 2005 and 2006 when the level of spam abuse encountered in alt tags – entire paragraphs of text blindly copied and pasted – led to Google and the rest of the search engines to discount them and look at site text instead.

Consider the benefits of good alt and title text. They:

- enhance the browsing experience of visitors with disabilities who rely on their special browsers to read to them pages which they cannot see and the different page elements (such as pictures and links)

- increase your page's keyword density score and relevancy for your targeted keywords, as described earlier in this chapter

- provide valuable information to all your visitors with descriptive link titles and descriptive text about other page elements.

For your information

When writing alt tags, be succinct. On occasion some web browsers will crash if the alt text has too many characters. While completely detailing what is in the image might be ideal, this is not the purpose of the alt tag. The reason for the alt tag is to put the image in context with regard to the rest of the page. The longest alt tag you use should not be longer than 64 words.

On the opposite side of the scale; don't make the alt tags so short that they are of no use at all. The alt tags should contain enough information for people who can't see the images to understand what the particular image represents. The same goes for search engines.

Be aware of the role alt tags play in SEO. Use clear and concise alt tags that relate to the keywords on the page to maximise the effectiveness of your alt tags with regard to SEO.

Don't write alt tags purely for search engine bots – alt tags should be written for the user first, and the search engine second.

Ensure your alt tags will be indexed by Google

▶

The best results by far happen when the alt tags you employ compliment the page's content. The reason for this is because Google employs a complex algorithm designed to mimic human intelligence. A human user coming across your site will immediately be able to spot that you are trying to skew the organic search engine page results by cheating. All they would have to do is mouseover your pictures, look at the alt tags and compare them to the content on the page and to the other elements on your site that describe what it does and what it is about.

The Google bot is not intelligent. It tries, however, to do the same thing as a human operator by carefully considering the alt tags, page content and site's overall content.

Google now indexes alt tags, but limits its indexing to just 125 characters. It possibly considers anything that goes over this number consistently, and by a lot, as search engine spam.

Here is how to ensure your alt tags will be indexed and that they really will make a difference.

Suppose you have a picture that shows a detached house for sale in Wilmslow, Cheshire, for £397,000, being sold by Mellor's Estate Agents.

Here's a bad example of what you could put in the alt tags: 'Large detached house for sale in Wilmslow, Cheshire, £397,000. Land for sale, house for sale, detached house for sale in Cheshire. Cheshire house estate agents house sale.'

Here's a good example: 'Wilmslow, Cheshire detached house for sale'. This is well below the 125-character limit and more consistent with what you would expect, in that it is a concise description, and so it will be indexed by the Google bot.

Creating alt tags for your site has to be as meticulous and well thought out a process as creating content for it. Get it right and, when it comes to the wire between your site and one of similar content and authority that has no alt tags, you will find your site ranks organically higher every time.

1 Make a list of all the pictures on every page of your website. Carefully create well thought out alt tags that describe each one in relation to the page content and your website's role.

2 If you are working in HTML rather than a content management system (CMS), make sure that the alt tags you drop in are in the Alt tags field rather than the Title field. Title fields are still ignored by many search engines, including Google.

3 Put the description of the picture in the field marked 'Alt'. Note that some CMS programs have begun to use the description 'Title' instead of 'Alt'. If in doubt add the same description to each.

For your information

Here's what your HTML alt tag code should look like:

```
<img src="mypic.jpg" width="50"
height="40" alt="Your 125 characters
maximum picture description here">
```

This will be added whenever you drop a picture in anywhere on your website.

What is Black Hat SEO (and how do you avoid it)?

▶

In the effort to optimise a website, every webmaster comes up against – sometimes by design and sometimes by accident – SEO techniques that are on the search engine's banned practises list.

The temptation is understandable. After all, you have worked hard, as a webmaster, on creating your website. You have put a lot of time, effort and money into its development and you want it to feature high on the organic search engine results page (SERPs). So you can, at times, be tempted to apply so-called Black Hat SEO techniques.

One particular favourite (and Black Hat SEO technique that you should never use) was to employ a clear 1 pixel image on your site. It was invisible to human visitors but had detailed, keyword-stuffed alt tags on it so search engines could index a site higher than its content really warranted.

Be warned – if you do anything like this today, your site will be instantly banned, so make sure you do not succumb to the temptation. Its success is short-lived and spending up to nine months outside a search engine's database is not going to help your online business.

Google and the other two major search engines (Yahoo! and Bing) are very strong in terms of their response to websites that are flagged up on their radar.

BMW wiped out by Black Hat SEO

Not too long ago (at the beginning of 2007, as a matter of fact), no less a firm than BMW had had its wrist slapped by Google for hiring a firm that used Black Hat SEO techniques.

BMW.de simply disappeared off Google's database like it never existed – and this applied to all its listings. A Google statement on the subject read. 'We can confirm that BMW.de has been removed from our search results. We never comment on the specifics of individual cases but we would stress that the quality of our index and search results is of the utmost importance to Google.'

At the same time, a Black Hat SEO firm called Traffic Power, which had huge corporate customers, disappeared off Google's listing, along with everyone on its client list, all 10,000 of them!

That is how seriously Google takes anything appearing to be Black Hat SEO and how swiftly it penalises it. Having said that, Traffic Power was able to grow and continue to grow and attract clients because its techniques worked and because it was there for years.

Black Hat SEO techniques

Black Hat techniques are transient. Google looks at them and adjusts its algorithm to discount them, whereas White Hat SEO techniques are permanent and produce lasting value.

The techniques that you must never employ on your website:

- **Invisible text** Never put white text on a white background. In fact, don't put even very light yellow text on a white background.

- **Cloaking** Google knows what's on your site because its bot has been there. Cloaking means showing one page to Googlebot and a completely different page to real human visitors. Google despises this activity and will actually ban sites that employ cloaking scripts.

- **Keyword stuffing** The engines want your pages to be natural. Finding every place possible to cram your keywords on your pages or writing a 'paragraph' of nothing but keywords – especially if they're repeated ad infinitum – is a big red flag raiser.

- **Doorway pages** A doorway page is a page built specifically for the purpose of ranking well in the search engines and has no real content of its own. It usually then links to the 'real' destination page or automatically redirects you there.

- **Spam** Spam has a special meaning with regards to SEO – that is, worthless pages with no content, created specifically for the purpose of ranking well in the engines. You think they have what you're looking for, but, when you get there, it's just a bunch of ads or listings of other sites.

What is Black Hat SEO (and how do you avoid it)? (cont.)

The point of all this is that, now you know what Black Hat SEO is, there really is no excuse for employing any. Whatever short-term gains you make will be lost soon enough – and it will be a permanent loss.

SEO basics

2

Introduction

The Web is the largest unified publicity forum that we have. Because everything that happens in it is visible, one of the key skills of SEO is understanding exactly *how* to look. This is important because it then allows us to realise just what we need to do when it comes to making our own websites visible, which is the primary aim of SEO.

In this chapter, you will learn some SEO basics and that SEO relating to visibility can also be employed to help you find out what your competitors are doing and what is being said about you and your online business.

What you'll do

Explore SEO options

Learn about meta tags and how to use them

Set up your meta tags

Learn about SEO and your Joomla site

Create a search engine-friendly site

Learn about SEO reputation management

Find out about five ways to manage negative content

Learn about SEO and ego searches

Learn how to set up an RSS ego search

Optimise your website with a two-minute guide on the basics

Exploring SEO options

When you optimise your website, you actually have more than just one option to choose from, in terms of that optimisation. For the website owner, there are different aspects of SEO.

- **Onsite SEO** This involves optimising your website by running a check through each of its pages and making sure that the meta tags are right (we shall see in detail shortly what they are and how you can best use them) and creating site content.

- **Offsite SEO** Publicity of your website and its content through the creation of articles and profiles in article aggregation sites or online profile sites such as AssociatedContent.com and Squidoo.com.

- **Search engine marketing** Marketing your site to search engines so that they can index it fast.

- **Social presence of your online business** A presence for your website on Twitter and Facebook.

- **Online publicity** Mainly by means of the release of online press releases (PRs).

- **An independent blog** A presence for your site on Blogger.com or Wordpress.com.

The line dividing search engine optimisation as a practice and online marketing as a discipline has been so eroded of late that it is impossible to tell the two apart. This is good news for you rather than bad. As a website owner, you will often find yourself wearing many different hats at different times of the day. Now, the marketer's hat and the search engine optimiser's happily coincide. Most of the activities, if not all, that you will undertake as part of the optimisation process for your website are also the ones you should be carrying out to successfully market your website online.

Meta tags

Meta tags are HTML codes that are inserted into the header on a Web page, after the title tag. In the context of SEO, when people refer to meta tags, they are usually referring to the meta description tag and the meta keywords tag.

The meta description tag and the meta keywords tag are not seen by users. Instead, the main purpose of these tags is to provide meta document data to user agents, such as search engines. In addition to the well-known meta description and meta keywords tags, there are other useful meta tags. These include the meta http-equiv, meta refresh, meta robots, meta copyright and meta author tags. These tags are used to give Web browsers and search engine spiders directions or data on various information.

Meta type	Description	What it looks like
Copyright	States the copyright of the site.	`<meta name ="copyright" content="© Copyright 2010 Yourcorp, Inc. All rights reserved." />`
Description	A two- or three-sentence description of the content of the page. Used by many search engines in the search results as the text under your link.	`<meta name="description" content="Your Description" />`
Keywords	A list of six to eight relevant keywords for this page. Largely abused so it's ignored by Google and most other engines.	`<meta name="keywords" content="your, keywords, here" />`
Geo Position	Attributes a specific geographical location to your site. It helps search engines, like Google, who display different results based on the location of the searcher.	`<meta name="geo.position" content="30.4363439; -97.7728595" />`

Meta tags and how to use them (cont.)

There are several 'tags' that go into the HTML code for a page of a website. These tags are placed between the `<HEAD>` and `</HEAD>`. They are invisible to the average person browsing the site, but are used by the search engines when they come crawling through your site and index the pages – a process called 'spidering'. The tags should be present on every page of a website. The most important tags are:

- the `<title>` tag
- the 'description' `<meta>` tag.

The 'keyword' `<meta>` tag used to be important but is virtually useless now. This does not mean you can ignore it, however. It is still useful and should, whenever it occurs, be filled in to describe what your page is about.

Meta tag check list

Although meta tags are not crucial these days, they continue to be a component of on-page SEO.

Here are the tasks to help you get it right:

1. Check to see your description is defined and it is describing your content (preferably a maximum of 25 words in your description tag).

2. Check to see that your keywords are defined and that they also list misspelling and typos.

3. Check to see your keywords are not repeated more than three times.

4. Preferably use no more than 1–3 main keywords and keyword phrases in your keyword tag.

First, set up your `<title>` tag. Our site would contain a `<title>` tag like this:

```
<title>The title of your website goes here</title>
```

What you put in here is based on the main keyword for your website. So, if your website is about selling ice to Eskimos, it should contain the words 'Ice to Eskimos' at least once. The description should not be more than 60 characters in length. In fact, if you can make it seven words or fewer (discounting words such as 'and' and 'for', which the search engines ignore anyway) you're better off. The `<title>` tag must also contain the main keyword phrase for which you are optimising that page. Google in particular places heavy emphasis on what is in your page's `<title>` tag. So does Bing.

Next, set up your `<meta>` keyword tag. Ensure that this contains the keyword phrases for the specific page you are on:

```
<meta name="keywords" content="use
the main keywords each separated by a
comma, blah, blah, blah">
```

Don't make this more than about 250 characters long, nor use the same keyword more than three times in it. Vary the capitalisation – don't use all capital letters unless the word is an acronym, such as 'SEO'.

Now, set up your `<meta>` description tag. This is a description of the page you are on:

```
<meta name="description" content="The
keyword for the main page we are on,
blah, blah, blah">
```

The description tag should describe the specific page it is on, not the whole website. This is the description of the page that shows up at the search engine when someone is lucky enough to find this page as a result of a search. Don't make the description more than about 200 characters long, make it descriptive and ensure that it contains your keyword phrases! Don't, though repeat individual keywords more than twice in any one meta tag because that can get a site banned from a search engine for something called 'spamdexing', which is 'spamming' the index of a search engine.

How to set up your meta tags

Timesaver tip

Don't obsess about the keywords tag. It is mostly disregarded nowadays due to abuse by people stuffing keywords that don't belong into it. You can almost skip it entirely without suffering any undue issues with your website, but it is a good discipline to include it.

2

How to set up your meta tags (cont.)

Next, put your keywords in the headings. These are used to separate the different sections of the content on a single page and are created using heading tags that look like this:

```
<H4>Put keywords in headings</H4>.
```

These 'headings' make your browser display the text larger and set it aside from the rest of the text, on its own line. Search engines will look for and index your headings when they index the pages on your site, so your headings should also contain the main keyword phrases for your site, like this:

```
<h1>Main keyword in heading</h1>
<h2>Main keyword and subheading</h2>
<h2>Main keyword and another subheading</h2>
<h2>Main keyword and the final subheading of
your text</h2>
```

and so on, through as many headings (in this case, products for sale) as you can think of that you want to include on that page. Such headings are weighted heavily by search engines – indeed, many of them use a formula that likes the keywords in headings more than elsewhere on a site, so don't neglect them. Use them to set off areas of text, in the same way that the pages in this book are divided up by headings.

Headings and Web design

Some people detest using headings because they tend to be big, clunky elements in Web designs and they can add a lot of space, lengthening the page. You can easily bypass this using a simple inline style command, like this:

```
<H1 style="margin-bottom: 0px; font-
size: 12px;">This produces a small heading with no
space after it!</H1>
```

The beauty of this is that it will still be recognised as a heading by the search engines as they tend to read the heading tags rather than look at the size of the text or the spaces.

That's it! You are done.

If you have a dynamic website, you will be using a control panel such as those offered by WordPress or Joomla to run it. The task of adding meta tags to each page on your site is very easy with these as they have been designed specifically to help non-technical users carry out technical tasks.

In the screenshots, you can see what the content management system (CMS) offered by Joomla looks like. Those of you who still use a program such as Dreamweaver to update your website will need to look for the meta tags command in its settings.

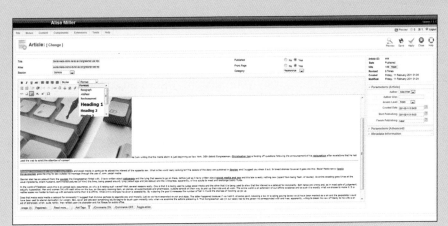

The screenshot above shows the administrative side of the CMS with an article about to be published. On the right hand side we can see how easy it is to put in a description and keywords.

The award-winning Joomla CMS makes the task of creating H tags in a title as easy as highlighting a line of text and choosing the size from a drop-down box. The screenshot below shows how easy it is to choose H tags for the headings.

Creating a search engine–friendly site

▶

?

Did you know?

The core of a website's optimisation relies on the ability to create fresh content regularly.

Many a perfectly designed website has fallen short of its SEO potential because the designers and the site owner failed to plan for the creation of fresh content all the time.

Discuss with your designers how you can best integrate a blog in your website or a news module designed to allow you to post news about your site easily.

The ideal time to start optimising your website is before it is even designed by paying attention to some very specific design characteristics and discussing them with your Web designer or Web studio at the creation stage.

The way your website will be designed will play a significant role in the level of search engine friendliness it displays. Even if your website has been designed and you have made some basic SEO mistakes, it may not be too late to rectify them now.

So, let's analyse where your attention should be in terms of creating a search engine-friendly site.

- **Frames** Frames are the kiss of death for many sites. They are difficult to index and search engine bots do not like them. At the design specification level, make sure that your website has no frames, but, if it does, ask your designers to rectify them.

- **Search engine-friendly URLs** If you have a dynamic website, you should ask your Web design studio to implement search engine-friendly URLs. This turns the string of 1s, 0s and dashes that dynamic websites automatically produce into person-readable copy, which search engines also like, and, often, turns a dynamic .php extension into an .html one.

- **Depth of archiving** Most websites give you some means of archiving material you place on them. The depth of the archiving is really important. Generally speaking, search engines will not index anything that is beyond three clicks deep, which means content accumulated on your site that should be helping your SEO will start to show up in deeper pages on the Google Index and this will seriously affect the way your website shows on organic search engine page results. To rectify this, you will need to make sure that any archiving system you implement on your website is readily available from any page where content is posted, which includes new as well as old content.

- **Graphic navigation elements** As mentioned before, but, for the record, search engines cannot see graphics. To them, the graphic elements that give your site its wow factor and entice your visitors are an obstacle, stopping them from indexing it properly. In order to avoid this, make sure you either have, instead of pretty menu item buttons, text navigational links on your site, as search engine bots can follow and index these or keep your menu buttons but *also* provide search engine-friendly text navigational links, usually at the very bottom of your website.

- **A heavy homepage** Flash technology elements and heavy graphics on your homepage will cause issues in terms of indexing as search engine bots do not like sites that take longer than a second to load. The problem here is connection speed. If your connection speed is faster, let's say, than your visitors', you will never know so, in order to decide, any homepage that is larger than 36 kbytes should be looked at carefully from a design and code point of view to see what can be done to make it lighter.

Jargon buster

Frames – Frames are an ill-advised way of creating websites so that each page loads other pages in it. For a good example of a website with frames, visit **http://download.oracle.com/javase/1.5.0/docs/api/** (it's a good safe site). The frames on this site are easy to recognise because you can see the scroll bars for each frame. You can set up frames with no scroll bars so that they all look like a single Web page. You see two frames on the left side, one at the top and one at the bottom, then a larger frame on the right-hand side. You can think of frames as internal browser windows because you can load a different Web page into each window. Actually, this site is like loading four Web pages instead of just one.

Bot – Short for robot. Often used to refer to a search engine crawler or spider.

Creating a search engine–friendly site (cont.)

■ **Keywords in the URL** If you have not got your website's keywords in the URL, you have just missed a *major* opportunity to score a goal with Google and the other two major search engines. Search engines look at a website's URL when they decide relevancy and organic placement, so, if you are selling oranges, for instance, and your website's URL is **ultimatetastes.com**, you have to work harder at getting your website placed high on search engine results for orange-related queries than one called, say, **ultimateoranges.com** will do.

The two diagrams below show the seven parts of a URL which a search engine sees and counts in its analysis of a domain name's ranking. The example used is one of a dynamic URL like those produced by Joomla or Wordpress websites. You can see the difference this makes from the first format of the dynamic URL as generated by the site's database and then the URL after it has been 'prettied up' to be more search-engine friendly.

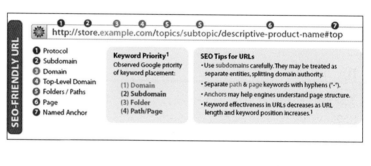

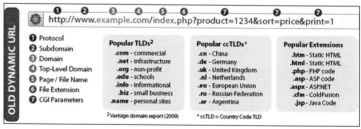

The fact that anyone can post anything online is a mixed blessing. Many companies have found, much to their horror, that others have posted half-truths or outright lies about them. What can you do if this happens to you or your company? That is where online reputation management and SEO comes in.

It is rare that a successful, long-standing company will not, at some stage, have some kind of negative feedback from a jealous competitor, dissatisfied client, prima donna who wants to look special or someone who simply wants to rock the boat.

With more and more user-generated content and social media opportunities, there is the danger that negative comments/ posts can find themselves in Google's top 10 or, even worse, above the fold when someone does a search for your company name, individual name, brand/product name or main keywords. At that point, they begin to cause damage to your reputation and need to be controlled, using the steps given.

SEO and reputation management

1 Identify the relevant keywords and keyword phrases. Often a company will check just their company name, brand name, product name and individual names. These are important, of course, as they refer specifically to the company, but you should also check other potential relevant keywords. A top 10 negative listing may be revealed when one of your main keyword phrases, is searched for, for example.

2 Next, formulate a strategy to push negative content down the Google index.

Did you know?

You can use meta tags to see what the title tag of a negative page is. Having checked your main reputation keywords – such as company name, brand and so on – look at the title tag of a negative page(s) to see if it contains other search terms that are relevant for your site and if they are also found in Google's top 10. Don't think automatically that it's just your company/brand/ product/individual keywords that are affected. In order to look at the title tag of a page, in Internet Explorer, right-click on the Web page and choose **View Source**. If you are using Firefox or Google Chrome, right-click **View Page Source**.

Five ways to manage negative content

▶

How to enlist Google's help

1. Carry out a Google search to find negative content which refers to your website or online business.

2. Make a note of the ranking of the negative content and then list all the results listed directly under the negative content on the Google search page. The aim is to find results which are below it in ranking but positive.

3. List all the web addresses (URLs) of the pages which feature positive content.

4. Now try to increase the ranking of the pages which have positive content by linking to them, sharing them amongst your friends and colleagues and asking clients, customers and friends to do the same.

5. Do this for each of the pages you have highlighted and you will start to see them rise above the page with the negative content. There are, of course, quite a few other factors which influence this, but by taking action you begin to set things in motion, in your favour.

■ **Bump up existing pages that have positive or neutral comments**

Not *all* the results in the top 20 will be negative. So, if, for example, the negative comment for your company's name is currently ranking fourth on Google, you need seven pages of positive or neutral content ranking above it to push it on to the second page where it is both less noticeable and will have a lot less impact on your online reputation.

■ **Create new content by means of articles, a new blog and so on**

First of all, check your 'about us', 'contact', 'our team' pages and so on. Make sure that you optimise them by adding, say, if the company name is a problem, the company name at the front of the title tag for each. This could then mean that you don't get just the one entry for your company name but two or more. This in itself pushes the offending page down one or more places.

You could also add new features, such as your own forum or blog, ensuring that your keywords are in the title tag for each. Write articles that could be seen as controversial or are in some way orientated towards getting others to link to them. This has the effect of not only boosting your own authority via external links, if that is a problem, but it may well also be syndicated on large websites (promote it as such) and, therefore, could result in a strong website taking up the article.

■ **Add new subdomains, sister domains (.co.uk, .info), other pages and so on**

A very effective strategy is to use subdomains. Google sees them as separate sites, but they do still carry the authority and trust of the root domain – 'My site name Internet Marketing' in Google.uk lists, in the first place, my forum (because it's the page most linked to); in the second place my actual home page; but in the third and fourth places are my subdomain xyz.mysitename-internet-marketing.uk, for example.

Subdomains are the third level domains that are used to organize your web site content. They are just like folders under your root directory. But they will have a special URL to access.

http://www.yoursite.com is the regular URL without a subdomain.

http://products.yoursite.com is a URL with subdomain 'products'. Here the .com is the first level domain, yoursite is the second level domain, products is the third level domain.

You do have to be sure, when you create a subdomain, that you do not just copy content from your main domain and it does have useful, unique content. It doesn't need 100 pages in it, either – ten or so pages per subdomain is fine. Do not overdo it, and if you can, create two to three subdomains.

Subdomains aren't the only answer, though. Maybe you already have other existing domains. If you do, check that these 'sister' domains are well optimised and well linked externally. If you don't have any other domains, then you can create new domains, ensuring the keyword you want to cover is in the domain name.

If you are going to create new domains, do not expect instant success. They will need their own link juice and tend to take a few months to even show up in the top 15. You will also need content for these pages, which should be different from what you already have on your main website.

■ Add content to external strong authority/trusted domains and use social media avenues

A really effective way to push negative pages down is to identify strong authority/trusted domains that allow you to pay to have user-generated content or entries posted on them.

If you do not have a Twitter account, get one and use your keyword in the username. Twitter, by the way, is very effective indirectly for SEO, but not in the sense of a direct linkage, as we shall see in Chapter 9.

Five ways to manage negative content (cont.)

Subdomains and how to create them

1. To create a subdomain go to the control panel provided by your hosting provider where your site is being hosted.

2. Log in your host panel. You will see a link Subdomains.

3. Enter a subdomain name. Create by clicking **Add**. Once a subdomain is added, it will be listed in the bottom three dropdown lists.

4. You can redirect your subdomain. Useful in redirecting separate subdomains to your affiliate products. That's it! You're done.

Five ways to manage negative content (cont.)

Add content to sites with a high profile on the Web

1. Go to each of the high profile websites (e.g. MySpace, Facebook, StumbleUpon, Squidoo, Hubpages) and create an account.

2. Write a short article or description for each one (try to make it as different as possible).

3. Link from your article or description to the positive pages you are trying to promote.

4. Use your site to also highlight the postings you have made and also link to the positive pages from your website for an added boost.

Consider MySpace and Facebook or other social bookmarking network entries, too. Also, of course, create interesting press releases, ensuring that your keywords are in the heading, and make sure to get a professional PR company to distribute them to as many press portals as possible. Last, but not least, don't forget to also link to these 'piggy back' pages from your own and external websites.

■ **Reduce the authority/trust of offending pages**

This is a tricky one. Often the reason a page ranks well has a lot to do with how and from whom it is linked. Therefore, check to see who is linking to the negative comment/ post page. A good way to do this is via search engines. In Yahoo!, type in the search mask for Yahoo:

link: **http://www.negativedomain.com/negativepage.htm -site:negativedomain.com**

This will provide you with a list of all pages that link to the negative page externally. Obviously, change the domain name wording in the address above and page name to the one relevant for you.

Once you have identified who links to this page you will have a clear idea of how easy or difficult it will be to manage them.

Keeping track of your competitors (and your own reputation) should be a standard weapon in your marketing arsenal. In the online world, no action takes place in a vacuum and, in every competitive business environment, what you do should always be informed by what is happening with those who are engaged in online businesses that are similar to yours. This is where ego searches come in.

Ego searches are free and simple searches designed to monitor blogs and news portals for mentions of your company, product, competitors or other specific keywords. Conducting ego searches not only allows you to stay informed but also maintain a strategic advantage over competing companies.

Creating an ego search is straightforward and, once you have done it, it should, ideally, always be there as a resource for you to use. That is why you need to use blogs and RSS feeds. Both of these are dynamically updated and Google indexed, so finding out what is happening is pretty easy. In order to run an ego search using blogs and RSS feeds, you need two things:

- An RSS reader (which will display the RSS and blog updates) – if you haven't got an RSS reader, Google has a free one that you can use (at: **www.google.com/reader/view**)

- An RSS aggregator – the Wikipedia definition of an RSS aggregator begins by saying: 'An **aggregator** or **news aggregator** or **feed reader** is a client software that uses a Web feed to retrieve syndicated Web content such as blogs, podcasts, vlogs, and mainstream mass media websites, or in the case of a search aggregator, a customised set of search results' (**http://en.wikipedia.org/wiki/News_aggregator**). You can check out an RSS aggregator at: **www.sharpreader.net**

SEO and ego searches

How to automate an ego search to happen daily

2

1 Go to Google Advanced Search (**http://www.google.com/advanced_search**) and select 'past 24 hours' in the date field. This will filter all web pages from Google search results that were indexed more than 24 hours ago.

2 Type your name enclosed in quotes in the search box – also include any common misspellings separated by the OR operator (e.g. – 'david amerland' OR 'davud amerland' OR 'david amberland'). Click **Enter**.

3 Copy the Google URL in the address bar and paste that into the search box at Page2RSS.com (**http://page2rss.com/**). This will create an RSS feed of your search results that you can subscribe to via email or in any news reader.

4 Now if there's a new web page that mentions your name or your company's name, it will be pushed to your inbox (or RSS reader) automatically.

How to set up an RSS ego search

1. Check that you have a Google e-mail account.

2. Go to Google Alerts (**www.google.com/alerts**) and simply conduct a keyword search of Google Alerts, specifying whether you are checking news or the entire Web for the search term you want.

3. Then, in the **Deliver to** field, choose **Feed**.

4. Every time a new article with that keyword appears in Google Alerts, the feed in your RSS reader will automatically update. You can then choose to be notified either via e-mail or the RSS feed on Google Reader.

Jargon buster

RSS (Real simple syndication, rich site summary or rich site syndication) – A Web feed format used to publish frequently updated material (such as blog entries, news headlines, audio and videos) in a standardised format that can be read by RSS readers across the Web.

Here is a two-minute guide on the basics for starting your onpage search engine optimisation on your website.

- Use a two- or three-word combination that best describes your site, its products or service as your *main* keyword. Research shows that 31 per cent of those who carry out an online search use two-word phrases in the search engine field. A further quarter of all those using search type a three-word combination. Just 19 per cent of users pin their luck on a single word.

- In the first instance, choose your keywords carefully and, if possible, go for a niche within your industry. If your site is new, going toe-to-toe with the big, established companies will only be disheartening.

- You are probably an expert in your industry. Be careful not to get carried away and choose a keyword that is so specialised no one but an expert will possibly use it. At the same time, do not use keywords that do not strongly relate to your site's content because you will start raising search engine red flags (alarms).

- Do not use keywords that may get you banned. Any high traffic keyword not related to the site could lead to it being banned, such as a video game website using keywords of the likes of 'Manchester United'.

- Do not use images with filenames or alt tags (alt attributes of img tags) as they may cause your site to be filtered or banned from search engines.

- Only use dynamic pages when it is required by the functionality of your site.

- Optimise each single page for a set of keywords, then repeat the cycle with new content.

- Organise your new content structure so that you do not bury old pages with new ones.

- Do not post half-finished or 'under construction' sites.

i 2

For your information

SEO is always about going the distance rather than getting there in a sprint. You may have not read any other chapter of this book yet but you could start to put what you have learnt into practice now.

SEO essentials

Introduction

The core of the success of your SEO will revolve around your ability to pick and then use the correct keywords for your website. In this chapter you will see just how important keywords are, how to analyse them, how to research them and then how to use them in order to optimise a website.

What you'll do

Learn about keywords and what they are

Learn how to research keywords

Learn how to use keywords in your content

Learn about keywords in description tags

Write clever description tags

Learn about a site's page rank and what it means

Keywords and what they are

When people are searching for information on the Web, they usually visit a search engine and type some words describing what they are looking for in the search box. The search engine then checks its database and returns the results, listing pages that relate to the words submitted.

So, how do you determine what keywords are relevant for your site? First, you need to put yourself in your potential customers' shoes to determine what words they would submit to the search engine when they are looking for you.

List these words and phrases, as they will form the basis for optimising your Web pages so

that they will rank higher on the search engines. The more specific your keywords the better. Remember that single-word keywords will have a lot more competition for top-ranking search results than phrases.

Don't expect the identification of your keywords and submission of your pages to the search engines to result in an immediate flood of traffic to your site. First, many of the search engines take a number of weeks to process your submission as they receive so many each day. Second, some search engines rank sites based on a number of factors, including popularity.

When you do keyword research, you're looking for words related to your business that have the following qualities:

- they will result in enough traffic to drive your income

- there is sparse competition, so you have a chance of showing up on page 1 of the search results

- if you're selling something, you want visitors who are looking to buy rather than just looking for general information.

With those goals in mind, start collecting your keywords. Begin with a broad general category, such as 'Internet marketing', 'dog training', or 'weight loss'. Then, think about the unique aspects of what your site offers. (You can work this from the other direction, too – find what people are looking for and figure out a way to offer it.)

Did you know?

Although there are hundreds of search engines, the only ones that really matter – in terms of the traffic they will send to your website – are Google, Yahoo! and Bing, in that order.

3

Timesaver tip

Keywords are the engine which drives your site forward. I often suggest two shortcuts to getting some great ones, fast:

1 **Ask for help** Talk to friends, colleagues or business partners and see which keywords they best associate your site with. Their insight often proves valuable.

2 **Google it up** What I love about Google is you can search for something and, as you type it, a bunch of popular searches come up that are similar to what you are typing. For instance, if you go to Google and start typing in 'goat's milk soap', a drop-down list shows related searches, like:

goat's milk soap benefits
goat's milk soap recipe
goat's milk soap babies
goat's milk soap base

So, now you have additional popular searches using 'goat's milk soap', but that are potentially less saturated. Do the same thing for keywords associated with your website.

With these two you have an almost instant way of generating relevant keywords that will help your website.

How to research keywords (cont.)

See also

Chapter 1, Creating a Google AdWords account

Maybe you want to home in on how to blog for money, housetrain puppies or build a sensible exercise routine. If your research suggests that those are still too large, keep narrowing your focus. Collect a *lot* of keywords.

This is, often, a hard task. Luckily there are some online tools that can help you and, even more luckily, they are totally free to use. There is, for example, the Google AdWords Keyword Tool. This is a powerful aid to researching, as well as appraising, keyword suggestions. It can save you valuable time by helping you find the many search terms, and their variations, that are relevant to what you want to do and are already used by online searchers.

You will notice that, at the top of the Keyword Tool, you can input not just a search term that you think is relevant to your website and you now want to research but also your website (if it has been built already). This helps Google to refine the terms it suggests by actually analysing your website first.

The next thing you should do is tick the box 'Only show ideas containing my search terms', which is directly under the field where you have typed in your suggested keyword.

Doing so will result in you being given keywords that are very specific to your search term. You can, if you want, leave this unticked. Google will then also suggest keywords that are related to your search term you may not have thought about. At this stage, it really is worth experimenting with both to see which one will work best for you.

You can see that I have used as a search term 'SEO'. If I were to leave the box below it unticked, this would allow Google to check its database and give me search terms that may be related to SEO but may not be directly linked to what I was thinking about.

The results are listed, but Google goes a step further and also gives me the number of searches that are made for a particular keyword each month, both globally (worldwide) and locally (in my case, the UK).

At this point it is worth mentioning that, if you have an AdWords account (you can sign up for one with Google even if you do not have any intention of buying AdWords advertising), the results will go into even greater depth for the search terms you have selected.

At the bottom of the Keyword Tool, you can (and should) refine the search of your keywords based on location (in this case, the UK) and language.

i

For your information

Develop your keyword strategy during the site design process when you are already focused on how to communicate the purpose of your website. Selecting the best keywords is much like writing an extremely short mission statement. After Google has suggested, ask yourself three basic questions:

1 What is the site's focus?

2 Why is the site's information valuable?

3 Who is your audience?

The answers to those questions will help you select appropriate keywords because they force you to think about how your site's content best serves its intended audience.

Be ruthless and discard any keywords which do not fit within the answers of the three questions you ask.

3

How to research keywords (cont.)

This is important to you as a webmaster because Google actually looks at its database of search queries in order to make the best suggestions possible for you. By specifying a location, you are directing Google to look at a particular part of its database that will have the most relevant search history for your purposes.

The thing to remember about keywords is that what you may think is relevant may not always appear that way to those who are looking to find your website. To be certain, although the Keyword Tool will have pointed you in the right direction, you really need to do a little more research. That is where Google's Wonder Wheel comes into its own.

To start it off, you need to first go to the Google Index relevant to you (at: **www.google.co.uk**). To illustrate how it is done, I have used my previous keyword – 'SEO' – again.

The moment I click **Search** or press **Enter** on my keyboard, the Google search results for that term appear and are general enough that there is a great deal of imprecision.

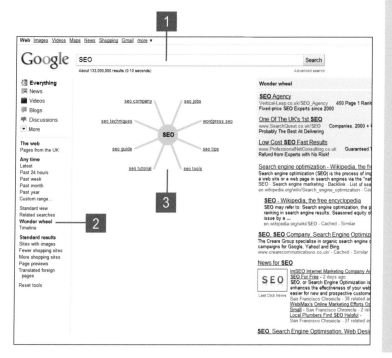

You can see that, right now, I have over 130 million results pages that I know are competing with me if I decide to go with that search term. I really do have to narrow it down further and, for that to happen, I need to understand how I could break down the search term and in what direction I want my focus to be.

On the left-hand side of a Google search page there are some additional options that will allow me to do just that. The one I am interested in is called Wonder wheel.

Accessing the Google Wonder Wheel

1. Type in a popular keyword which describes what your site does (i.e. SEO).

2. Look at the left-hand side bar of Google Search. Click Wonder wheel.

3. The Wonder Wheel is a visual presentation of the popular keyword you have typed into search and the different categories in which it appears. By looking at it in this way it allows you to begin thinking about how to best position your website.

How to research keywords (cont.)

The moment you click **Wonder wheel** you get a visual representation of how a search generates its results, based on categories of queries.

You can see from the screenshot that 'SEO' as a hub spikes off into different categories, ranging from 'seo techniques' to 'seo tools' and 'wordpress SEO'. If I had a website that specialised in SEO, I would, at this stage, start thinking about which of these specific categories I wanted my site to point towards.

For argument's sake, let's assume that I started to point my website towards 'seo techniques' as the most relevant to what I am offering. Instantly I can see options for further refinement. What's more, on the right-hand side, I can now see which of the 130 million plus pages that appeared before for my term 'seo' are now showing for 'seo techniques'.

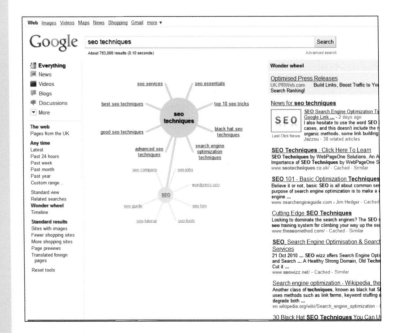

You can continue to drill down in this way for some time until you have the exact level of refinement that you think best reflects what your site does. At that point, you will have narrowed down the field so as to optimise your website and a clear direction regarding the keywords to associate with it.

Now that you have got your keywords, it is time to see just how we can best use them.

When it comes to optimising your website, there is a host of onpage items that you absolutely need to optimise for. These are not only *doable* by a novice SEO webmaster but are absolutely *essential*, so let's look at them one at a time.

■ **Keyword in URL** If you have no keywords in the URL of your website and no chance of getting them in there, you are missing a golden opportunity to promote your website organically.

Best practice: First word is best, second is second best, third is third best and so on.

■ **Keyword in title tag** Use your keywords in the title tag for your page.

Best practice: A title tag is between 10 and 60 characters long and has no special characters.

■ **Keyword in description meta tag** This shows that your content is now thematically linked and so are your keywords.

Best practice: Make this under 200 characters long. Google no longer relies on this tag, but will often use it.

■ **Keyword in keyword meta tag** This, again, is part of your thematic linking. Every single word you use in this tag **has to** appear in the body text of your page somewhere. If it does not, you will be penalised for spamming and irrelevance.

Best practice: Use fewer than ten words. Do not repeat words anywhere. Google, reportedly, no longer uses this tag, but others do.

■ **Keyword density in the body text of your page** Achieve 1 to 3 per cent (all keywords/ total words) density in your topic on the page. Some report topic sensitivity based on this, which means that the percentage for the keyword spamming threshold varies with the topic.

Best practice: To be on the safe side, keep well within the 5 per cent limit. Check the keyword density of your text before you drop it in at: **www.articleannouncer.com/tools/keyword.html**.

Keywords and how to use them in your content

3

For your information

To best employ keywords into your content:

1 Make sure the initial keyword is utilized once in the first 25 words of the document.

2 Contextually integrate the secondary keyword 1–2 times into the page.

3 Make sure the page has 500–750 word min. so that search engines have enough context to identify the pages primary and secondary topic.

4 Use both the singular keyword variation and the alternative variation in the title if possible (or in the title+meta tag) – such as keyword 1 in title, and keyword 2 (singular or plural in meta data).

5 Build internal links using the alternative keyword variations to supply the foundation of link flow.

Keywords and how to use them in your content (cont.)

ArticleAnnouncer™
Article Toolbox

Keyword Density Analyzer

Keyword research and analysis is an important step when writing your articles. Selecting the right keywords will help you to better define your target audience and increase your odds of gaining better search engine rankings and boosting your traffic.

Keyword density plays a major role. Once you have written an article, *cut-and-paste* your article below and also type in your target keywords. A keyword density analysis will be performed right away -- even without you pressing the "update" button.

This means, you can *tinker* around with various keywords *on-the-fly* and get immediate results on how it impacts your overall keyword density.

Tip: Try and vary your keyword density. As a general guideline, try to aim for anywhere between 2% to 7% keyword density.

How to use this tool:

Step 1... Type in the keyword(s) you want to check
Step 2... Cut-and-paste in the article text that you want to analyze

Keyword One:	SEO	**Ratio:** 5.1	%
Keyword Two:	SEO Technique	**Ratio:** 1.7	%
Keyword Three:	SEO tools	**Ratio:** 1.7	%

Cut-and-paste your article below:

This is a practice SEO Text designed to test keyword density for a specific number of SEO techniques and SEO-related text. Keyword density is just one of the many SEO tools available to the novice webmaster looking to best optimize their website and avoid incurring search engine penalties due to excessive usage of specific keywords in the copy which goes on their website. By remaining within the acceptable range he ensures that his keyword density is seen as being totally natural and not forced the way it would have been had he input 'SEO Techniques', for instance at every possible opportunity he found, without any regard for the final user experience (i.e. the online visitor coming to your website). Like most good SEO tools excessive use of any kind of keyword will most likely cause more harm than good and undo much of the hard work which goes into optimizing a website.

As you can see in the example used in the screenshot, I have optimised my text for three specific search terms – 'SEO' (a generic one), 'SEO Technique' and 'SEO Tools'.

■ **Keyword in H1, H2 and H3 headings**. Use bold text and relevant keywords in your H1, H2 and H3 headings on your page.

Best practice: Choose your headings carefully to appeal to both human readers and search engine bots.

■ **Individual keyword density** When it comes to individual keywords on your Web page as a whole, it is best to keep them between 1 and 6 per cent of the total number of words used.

Best practice: Check your Web page's keyword density: at: **www.seocentro.com/tools/seo/keyword-density.html**.

Keyword Density Tool

Menu
» Home
» SEO Archives
» SEO Articles
» SEO Services

SEO Tools
» Meta Tag Analyzer
» Rank Checker
» Keyword Analyzer
» Link Popularity
» Search Saturation
» Keyword Suggestion
» Keyword Density
» PageRank Check
» DC PageRank Check

Promotion Tools
» Bookmark Buttons
» RSS Subscribe Buttons

Online Tools
» Server Headers Check
» IP to Country

🔖 BOOKMARK

Keyword Density analysis tool to help webmasters analyze the keyword density from their web pages and include a tag cloud for easy display of the most important keywords from your site. Keyword density is the measurement in percentage from the number of times a keyword or phrase appears compared to the total number of words in a web page.
Bookmark this page!

Check your keyword density?

example: **http://www.host.com or http://www.host.com/index.html.**

http://_____ URL

Elements to include?
☑ Include Title ☑ Include Description
Include numeric keywords?
○ Yes ● No

`4 4 2 8`

Please enter the **access code** as displayed above.
_____ Access code

Submit

■ **Choose your keyword font size** Google treats 'Strong the same as bold, italic is treated the same as emphasis'.

Best practice: Find ways to use bold text and italics on your Web page without making it look like a dog's dinner!

■ **Keyword proximity (for 2+ keywords)** Google checks adjacent words and words in the same sentence in order to see if there is contextual support for the main keyword.

Best practice: Directly adjacent is best as it has the greatest effect in terms of SEO.

■ **Keyword phrase order** This is a really obvious and yet often people make mistakes. In the drive to include keywords in the text way too often, you forget to include phrases that *exactly* match the query searchers are likely to make.

Best practice: Make sure that you include at least one phrase that exactly replicates the search query those looking for the information you provide will make.

■ **Keyword prominence** *Where* your keywords appear in the text on your page is key to the importance search engines will give them. Make them bold and place them near the top and you immediately increase the weighting search engines will give your Web page for those keywords.

Best practice: Think carefully about where on the page you will place your keywords and try to find a way to give them prominence in a natural way.

For your information ⓘ

When you are looking for traffic which is suitable to convert into paying customers exact keywords is always better than approximate.

For instance, if you are selling in a competitive field, like SEO, and you are an expert at running pay-per-click (PPC) campaigns, it will serve you best by far to optimise your website for the keywords 'PPC SEO' rather than the more generic 'SEO'.

The trade-off of time (as it takes longer to do) for quality will always pay off in the long term.

3

Keywords in description tags ▶

Meta tags were the original way to tell search engines what your page was about. You'd add a description and a number of keywords into your meta tags and a search engine would come along to index your page, read these words and file your site under them.

This worked fine for a while, but it couldn't last. It wasn't long before webmasters with no scruples saw an opportunity to gain favour with the search engines by adding in keywords that did not pertain to the content of their pages. Various tactics were thought up to in order to be ranked higher for certain keywords and, as a result, an entire industry sprang up to optimise search engine positioning. It was, in effect, cheating and 'keyword spamming', as it was called, became a serious problem for search engines, which vainly attempted to add filters that would notice when a webmaster was loading up on the wrong keywords.

Google changed all of that by using not the meta tag description of a page but its content. This worked so well that the rest of the search engines followed suit, ignoring meta tags and reading, instead, the keywords content of a page. Google, however, while still ignoring meta tags in terms of keywords, now does pay attention to the description tag.

The description tag is used by about half of the major search engines (the other half showing an excerpt from the page). It is a short summary of the content of the page and looks like this:

```
<meta name="description" content="This
page is about SEO, with particular
emphasis on SEO Techniques">
```

Your description needs to include some of your best keywords (as these are highlighted in the results), but it must also still . be readable by a person. If your descriptions are just a list of keywords, few people will click your link. You have to write with an eye to creating a balance between keywords and promotion.

As you can see in the screenshot, the description tag is what shows up on the Google search page when searching for the term 'seo techniques'. The quality of that description often makes all the difference between human visitors bypassing your listing and clicking on someone *else's* and clicking on it in order to visit *your* website.

Keywords in description tags (cont.)

3

Writing clever description tags

The description tag for your website is every bit as important as an advert. As it appears on the 'snippets' displayed by Google and other search engines when they show your site on their results pages, it fulfills the same role as an advert in the online visitor's mind.

The description tag

- identifies a need the visitor may have

- provides a solution

- closes the loop by telling him or her where to get it from.

Spend as much time as you can on writing your description tag for your page. Remember that your description meta tag should be no longer than 160 characters. To create it, experiment with a few sentences and try them out on yourself and friends to see which works best.

Here's an example of a badly written snippet.

REDACTED.com: **Harry Potter** and the Prisoner of **Azkaban** (Book 3 ...
REDACTED.com: **Harry Potter** and the Prisoner of **Azkaban** (Book 3): Books: JK Rowling,Mary GrandPré by JK Rowling,Mary GrandPré.
www.redacted.com/**HarryPotterPrisonerAzkaban**/path/path/path/docname.html - 193k - Cached - Similar pages

You can see that neither the title nor the description following underneath does much in terms of enticing online visitors to click on it.

A better snippet is this one.

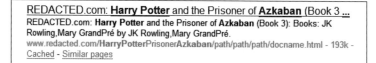

Google Video
Search and browse all kinds of videos, hosted on sites all over the web, including **Google**, YouTube, MySpace, MetaCafe, GoFish, Vimeo, Biku, and Yahoo **Video**.
video.google.com/ - 108k - Cached - Similar pages - Note this

Both the title and description in the second example tell online visitors, at a glance, what they are looking at and why they should click on it.

PageRank was the original thinking that became part of the Google search engine core code when Larry Page and Sergei Brin first published a paper on about a different type of search engine at Stanford University. The search engine that they initially started to create was intended to index the (digital) works held in Stanford University's library.

PageRank (PR) is Google's way of measuring your ranking in terms of links to your site from other sites, based on both their quantity and quality. Google page ranking varies from 0 (terrible) to 10 (ideal). The most basic way to achieve a good page ranking is to have lots of quality websites linking to you – it is almost like a vote of confidence for your site's content and its authority.

If you have lots of links from sites that themselves have low rankings, they will do very little for your page's rank. Even a few links from other sites with good page rankings, however, can make a difference. That doesn't mean you should cancel existing links, though, they still have some value.

Your page's rank is a good indicator of how important your website is in the eyes of a search engine. Ideally, you want to rank 4 or above.

A site's page rank and what it means

How to check a website's pagerank

1 Go to http://www.prchecker.info.

2 In the field box provided put in the URL of the website you want to check the PageRank of.

3 Click **Check PR**.

4 The software will now query the Google database and return with a value which will range from a minimum of '0' to a maximum of '10' for that particular website. The PageRank (PR) value of a website is a way of testing the effectiveness of its SEO. It is also used as a means of finding suitable sites to advertise on. The PR value is an indication of the importance of a website in the eyes of Google.

3

A site's page rank and what it means (cont.)

A little while back, having a high page rank was a sure fire way to ensuring that your website was placed advantageously on the search engine results pages. All this changed in 2007 when abuses (and even fake page ranks) made Google filter it out and discount it.

There are now two different types of page rank. There is the true page rank of your site, which is calculated on a daily basis by a Google algorithm. This allows the search engine to know exactly where to place your website on its results pages. That ranking and the precise way in which it is calculated remain closely guarded secrets.

Websites with a high PR are more trusted by online visitors and, when it comes to advertising, they attract higher prices than do those with a low PR.

According to Google:

PageRank reflects our view of the importance of web pages by considering more than 500 million variables and 2 billion terms. Pages that we believe are important pages receive a higher PageRank and are more likely to appear at the top of the search results.

PageRank also considers the importance of each page that casts a vote, as votes from some pages are considered to have greater value, thus giving the linked page greater value. We have always taken a pragmatic approach to help improve search quality and create useful products, and our technology uses the collective intelligence of the web to determine a page's importance.

A site's page rank and what it means (cont.)

?

Did you know?

PageRank is a link analysis algorithm, named after Larry Page – one of the founders of Google. It is used by the Google search engine and assigns a numerical weighting to each element of a hyperlinked set of documents, which is what websites are on the worldwide web, with the purpose of 'measuring' its relative importance within the set.

3

SEO and search engine marketing (SEM)

4

Introduction

SEO and search engine marketing (SEM) are two different sides of the same coin. In this chapter, you will learn what the difference is between the two and how and when to use each. You will also learn about the different options available to you when you want to achieve visibility for your website and time is against you.

What you'll do

Learn about search engine marketing channels

Learn about Facebook and Google ads

Set up a Facebook ad

Set up a Google AdWords PPC campaign

Create your ad group

Check your website's listings

Get your website indexed by Google in less than 12 hours

Learn what to do if your site has not been indexed properly

Learn about domain name indexing – www versus http://

Search engine marketing channels ▶

Search engine marketing (SEM) is everything that can be done to utilise the technology of search engines with the goal of promoting a website and increasing its traffic – its 'stickiness', as its called – and, in the case of sites that promote a business (or are a business), increase profits. Most SEO activities are a subset of SEM because, strictly speaking, a website is marketed to search engines so that they can index it better.

Aspects of SEM that I would consider to be outside the realm of search engine optimisation include paid inclusion and traditional ads – pay-per-view (PPV) and pay-per-click (PPC) varieties on Facebook and Google, for example. We shall look at each of these in turn.

Paid inclusion

This is simply the practice of paying a minor search engine or directory to add a site to its database immediately, rather than set up the site so that it will be found by the search engine spiders on its own. In the case of some search engines and directories, paid inclusion is the only way to ensure that your site is listed. For others, it's presented as an option. If you're willing to pay, your site will be listed sooner. It's also a useful practice if you wish to make frequent changes to your content, because your site will be spidered more often and you will be able to test how changes affect your ranking. This is also useful if you have a niche business that is served by a particular search engine or directory. One example is The Teddy Bear Search Engine (and Directory) which lists only teddy bear websites (**www.teddybearsearch.com**). Another – a little more relevant to our needs – is I Need Hits (**http://ask.ineedhits.com**), which provides results to the Teoma, Ask Jeeves and HotBot search engines. The only way to be listed in the Teoma index is through paid inclusion. This is one search engine that doesn't have a free add URL page any more.

It is valid here to consider whether or not paid inclusion in a particular search engine confers any advantages in ranking on its index. The emphatic answer – according to the search engines that accept paid inclusion – is a definite 'No!' Just like going private in medicine, paid inclusion, in niche search engines, speeds up the length of time it takes to become indexed and gives some additional reporting capabilities that those which have not paid, obviously, do not get.

The benefits are:

- on submission, your pages will make it on to the Teoma and Ask Jeeves indices within seven days

- your pages are respidered every seven days

- the term of the pay inclusion program is 12 months

- reporting services are included, such as click-through reporting.

Did you know?

If you want visibility for your website fast, then you have to pay. This includes paid inclusion in directories (such as the Yahoo! Directory) and Google Ads, as well as PPC in Yahoo! and Bing. If you are running a site that faces any of the following constraints, it makes sense to set aside a marketing budget and buy some advertising:

- your site is new and you want to attract traffic as soon as possible

- you have a time-sensitive offer that needs to be seen

- you are in a trading period that itself is a bottleneck, such as Christmas or summer sales

- if you have been knocked off Google's top three pages and need to maintain momentum while you give time to your SEO efforts for them to take off.

Jargon buster

Click-through – The process of clicking through an online advertisment to the advertiser's destination.

Traditional ads (PPV and PPC)

This involves placing paid advertising on the search engine result pages (SERPs). Normally, these ads appear as a result of the keywords entered into the search engines and you are charged based on the number of impressions – that is, appearances – of the ad. In other words, you pay whether the ad sends anyone to your website or not. These ads are normally taken on portals or high-traffic websites where the exposure is likely to bring in some traffic and where

Search engine marketing channels (cont.)

brandbuilding (making your website visible) is every bit as important as bringing traffic to your website. Ads like this are often called pay-per-view (PPV) ads.

The principle of PPV ads is websites that have high levels of traffic or companies which have some means of attracting eyeballs by disseminating free software (such as that which allows you to watch free digital TV channels on your desktop) then serve passive ads, meant only to be viewed.

Did you know?

Pay-per-view (PPV) advertising is intended to put your brand in front of a large number of people. This works if you are interested in creating brand awareness and follow it up with other campaigns that are intended to lead to action. Brand awareness leads to the uptake of different services or products united by a common brand. It can also help to deliver a larger slice of the market than would be the case if it were not employed.

Pay-per-click (PPC) ads

Pay-per-click (PPC) ads are simple enough to look at – they're text-only. PPC ad campaigns are completely controlled by the advertiser. You decide which keywords should bring up your ads, you write the copy and you decide how much you want to pay. Also, as the name indicates, you only pay for an ad when someone clicks it and is brought to your site.

There are three main networks of PPC ads: the biggest fish in the pond, Google with its AdWords program, Yahoo!, which serves its own ads in a similar scheme via Overture (which it owns) and Bing, which has its own set up. Each of these has its own advantages and disadvantages in terms of cost and reach, so you will need to think very carefully about the target customers you may want to reach. In every case, however, you will need to be prepared to spend a great deal of time (and money) monitoring and adjusting your campaign so as to get the best out of it.

The Google AdWords program is designed to give you flexibility as well as reach. It offers text-based as well as graphics-based ads that can be delivered in the paid column on the right-hand side of the search engine results pages as shown.

Jargon buster

Pay-per-click (PPC) – an Internet marketing formula used to price online advertisements. In PPC programs, the online advertisers will pay the Internet publishers the agreed on PPC rate, regardless of whether a sale is made or every time the advert displayed is clicked by a viewer or not. Also called cost-per-click (CPC).

Pay-per-view (PPV) – Another Internet marketing formula used to price online advertisements. In PPC programs, the online advertisers will pay the Internet publishers the agreed on PPV based on the number of times their advert is displayed. Also called pay-for-impressions (PFI).

4

Search engine marketing channels (cont.)

Alternatively, as shown, they can serve them on websites that have AdSense (the flipside of the AdWords program, which allows website owners to serve Google Ads and get a slice of the PPC cost).

i For your information

PPV – also known as buying or paying for impressions – allows you to set up an advert that can be either text-based or graphics-based and pay a specific sum per impression. Portals such as ZDNet (**www.zdnet.co.uk**) can put your advert in front of nine million monthly users. In the steps given in the following sections, you will see how to set up PPV campaigns with the biggest players in the business – Facebook and Google.

Ads on Facebook appear primarily down the right-hand side of the page. Go to anyone's profile and you'll usually see three ads. A large portion of them tend to be for quasi-junk – games, dating services and free iPods, so the local business ads often stand out.

These ads are created in Facebook's self-service advertising platform. All the self-service ads follow this same format – a short headline, small picture and longer piece of text below.

Advertising on Facebook can work for almost any type of business. They're useful for creating awareness, can be used to directly generate leads and are great for increasing the fan count on your Facebook page.

Setting up a Facebook ad

1. To get started, go to **www.facebook.com/advertising** – if you don't have a Facebook account, you'll be asked to create one as part of the ad setup process. There are three sections on the ad creation page: Design Your Ad, Targeting and Pricing and Scheduling.

2. In the first section, **Design Your Ad**, fill in the **Destination URL** box. You can use your website's homepage or may do better with a page specifically designed for Facebook visitors. Directly beneath the Destination URL is a link to 'advertise something I have on Facebook'. If you have a Facebook page set up, click this link to advertise your page.

3. Next, complete the **Title** box. If you're advertising a Facebook page, this will automatically default to your page's title. For anything else, you can choose what you like – a descriptive or promotional title will usually work better than just your business name.

Setting up a Facebook ad (cont.)

4 Then we come to the **Body Text** box. Filling this in is like writing any advertisement. You do have a nice amount of space (much more than with search engine advertising, for instance), although sometimes shorter text will prove more effective.

5 Lastly in this section, there is a box for uploading an **Image**. This is very important! The image generally has the largest impact on your ad's effectiveness. Many companies use their logos, but it's unlikely this will be the best choice (unless, possibly, you are looking to drive general brand awareness). You want something that stands out. Some things to try include using people, something creative or images that just 'pop' when your eye crosses over them. Remember that the picture will be small – it is only 110 × 80 pixels in size. If you don't have enough images of your own, you can purchase them from an online photolibrary such as iStockphoto.com (at: **www.istockphoto.com**).

Setting up a Facebook ad (cont.)

6 The second section is **Targeting** and Facebook's platform allows for some pretty amazing targeting.

7 Start by choosing the **Location** you want to target. An obvious choice for local businesses, you can get as specific as a particular city. As you update any of your choices, the Estimated Reach box on the top right-hand side automatically updates, alerting you to the potential target audience for your ad.

8 Then you complete the **Demographics** options. Choose an age range and sex. As we'll discuss later, you might want to create multiple ads to test different combinations.

9 The third option in this section is **Likes & Interests**, which can be a gold mine if used correctly. You can target users by interests they have entered on Facebook. If you type in job titles, this box will allow you to target by job as well. If you can think of things that your customers might like, your ad will be much more effective, although this will limit the overall reach.

Setting up a Facebook ad (cont.)

10 The **Connections on Facebook** section is helpful if you have a busy Facebook page. You can use it to increase your 'Likes' count by targeting those who are not currently connected to your page or increase engagement by targeting people who already are connected. Targeting friends of your connections can be an especially cheap way to add more 'Likes'.

11 You'll have to click **Show Advanced Targeting Options** at the bottom of the **Connections on Facebook** section to 'see Advanced Demographics and Education & Work'. These provide a wide range of targeting options, including birthdays, sexual preference, relationship status, education, language and workplace. For some companies, these are very useful – anyone in the wedding industry, for instance, so that they can target users with a relationship status of 'Engaged'.

12 The third and final section is **Campaigns**, **pricing and Scheduling**.

13 You'll need to create a new **Campaign Name** and set a daily **Budget**. You can schedule the campaign to run forever or set particular dates on which you want it to run, which is great if you have a special offer going.

14 Facebook will automatically set a Max Bid. To refine this, just enter your own bid in the box option. You can use **Suggested Bid (Simple Mode)** if this is just a small test, but, if you're going to be spending any significant money, be sure to keep a daily check on this (Facebook files a detailed report that you can access via your ad account with them).

15 Facebook is unique in that it allows you to set up a PPV ad campaign or a PPC one from the same ad. You simply have to choose by selecting the right option in the final step. Should you ever need to change this in the future, you can go back, duplicate the ad and change the way you have decided to pay for it or simply edit the same ad.

Once you have the campaign set up, you'll have to enter credit card information. Initially you'll be prevented from spending a huge amount per day, but this will increase after Facebook receives a few payments (they automatically charge your card after a predefined amount of spend). Your ad won't start to run until it has been approved, which generally takes a few hours.

Setting up a Google AdWords PPC campaign

When it comes to writing and placing Google AdWords ads successfully, the key is to make sure that you create very targeted ad groups around similar keywords. I recommend creating lots of different ad groups rather than one big ad group with piles of keywords. You can then create precisely targeted landing pages for each ad group. Not only will you get a better click-through rate with this technique (because the ad and landing page will be so relevant to each other, people will think, 'That's what I'm looking for!') but also *Google* will see your landing page as more relevant, so you'll achieve a lower minimum cost per click.

1. To create a new keyword-targeted campaign, log in to your AdWords account and click **Create your first campaign**.

2. Choose **English** as the language for the campaign.

3. Choose which countries to target. I suggest starting with the UK, USA, Canada, New Zealand, Australia and Ireland, if you are targeting a global English-speaking market, or just the UK if you are just after local business. Don't take the easy way out here and target 'All countries and territories', because not every country is equal in terms of profitability. For instance, you might get 1000 clicks from India but no conversions, so it would be easy to assume from those results that the search term isn't profitable.

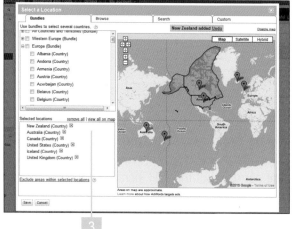

4

Networks and devices

Networks ⑦   ⦿ All available sites (Recommended for new advertisers)
         ◯ Let me choose...

Devices ⑦   ⦿ All available devices (Recommended for new advertisers)
         ◯ Let me choose...

Bidding and budget

Bidding option ⑦   Basic options | Advanced options
         ⦿ Manual bidding for clicks

         ⚲ You'll set your maximum CPC bids in the next step.

         ◯ Automatic bidding to try to maximize clicks for your target budget

Budget ⑦   UK£ [10] per day (Format: 25.00)
         Actual daily spend may vary. ⑦

⊞ Position preference, delivery method (advanced)

5

6

Ad extensions

You can use this optional feature to include relevant business information with your ads. Take a tour

Location ⑦   ☑ Extend my ads with location information
         ☐ Use addresses from a Google Places account ⑦
         ☐ Use manually entered addresses ⑦

Product ⑦   ☑ Extend my ads with relevant product details from Google Merchant Center

         You don't have access to any Google Merchant Center accounts.

Sitelinks ⑦   ☑ Extend my ads with links to sections on my site
         You can enter up to 10 additional links that may be shown with your ad. Additional links will only be shown for the single top-ranked ad for a given user search. Additional links are more likely to appear the higher the quality of the ad, and may not always be shown for every top-ranked ad. Learn more

         Link text: 35 max   Destination URL: 1024 max

Link 1: [   ]   http:// ▾ [   ]   Remove
Link 2: [   ]   http:// ▾ [   ]   Remove
Link 3: [   ]   http:// ▾ [   ]   Remove
Link 4: [   ]   http:// ▾ [   ]   Remove

         + Add another

Phone ⑦   ☑ Extend my ads with a phone number

         Country or territory [United Kingdom   ▾]
         Phone number [   ]

         This ad extension works with location extensions. Learn more

Setting up a Google AdWords PPC campaign (cont.)

4 Choose to display on **All available sites** and **All available devices** for maximum exposure (the latter is useful as tablets and smartphones have overtaken PCs and laptops in numbers).

5 Select your budget – I suggest that you start with what you think is reasonable rather than what Google suggests (such as £10 per day).

6 Refine your ad with ad extensions. Google allows you to serve ads with extreme local relevancy, so, even if you are using Google ads to target customers living within a ten-mile radius of your place of work, you can do so with all the options available to you on the ad extensions menu. It is even possible to link the ad to different sections on your website and show your phone number to local customers.

4

Setting up a Google AdWords PPC campaign (cont.)

7 Next, click **Edit** to decide if you want your ad to always appear, appear only at certain times of the week or on certain days.

8 Finally, select to which demographic it will be shown by clicking Edit. It makes perfect sense, for instance, to want to show an ad on dirt bikes to an age group of between 25 and 40 more than 55 to 70.

For your information

You should, whenever possible, have separate campaigns for content and search. This is definitely a best practice and should be adhered to. One thing you will notice is that the click through rate (CTR%) on a content campaign is drastically lower than something you will see with pure search.

There are also many types of keywords you might want to add in a content campaign that have no place in search (like complementary products), and the reverse is true too. You would probably never want to include brands or competitor names in a content campaign.

Ultimately, these are effective but very different types of advertising, and need to be managed separately. So if you are creating a PPC campaign, you should create a specific landing page for it in order to increase the return on your investment (ROI).

An ad group is a general description of your ad and it has its own set of keywords. When you only had one ad then the keywords for your ad and ad group are exactly the same. You may, however, want to create two or more ads about the same product (maybe because there are seasonal variations, or even to test different wording) – your keywords for each ad will then be slightly different.

◀ **Creating your ad group**

Your ad group will then contain more than one ad and its set of keywords will contain all the keywords you have chosen for each ad you have created. An ad group allows you to get an overview of an ad's performance and see how different sets of keywords perform against each other, quickly.

Make sure that you choose a headline and descriptions containing your keywords and, like any advert, go through the cycle of identifying a problem the people you are targeting have, providing a solution and giving them the means to getting it. Here are some tips for a well-written Google ad.

- Always include your main keyword in both the title and description. Then when someone searches for that keyword phrase, the matching words in your ad will appear in bold, which makes it even easier for people to see the ad's relevancy to what they are looking for.

- Be sure to capitalise the first letter of each word in the display URL because it's easier for people to read. I've tested this over 50 times and, in about 49 of those tests, the capitalisation made a noticeable difference to the click-through rate.

- The *display* URL can end differently from the *real* URL, as long as the first part of the website address is the same. For example, if the *real* website address is **http://YourproductSiteSpecialOfferPage.com**, then you're allowed to write the *display* URL as **http://YourproductSite.com** for memorability.

Creating your ad group (cont.)

1. Sign to your Google AdWords account and click **Create an ad group**.

2. Choose your keywords. To begin with, a list of one to ten similar keywords and keyword phrases will do just fine. I don't recommend that you have more than ten in your first few campaigns.

3. You can, if you like, ask Google to give you an estimated traffic summary for your keywords, which will help to give you an idea of how much you will spend.

√ Select campaign settings   ⟩ Create ad group

Create ad group

Name this ad group

An ad group contains one or more ads and a set of related keywords. For best results, try to focus all the ads and keywords in this ad group account.

Ad group name: MY Ad Group Name

Create an ad

◉ Text ad   ○ Image ad   ○ Display ad builder   ○ WAP mobile ad

To get started, just write your first ad below. Remember, you can always create more ads later. Help me write a great text ad.

Headline	My great website
Description line 1	Best product ever
Description line 2	at the best price
Display URL ⑦	www.mysite.com
Destination URL ⑦	http:// [▼] www.mysite.com/myproductpage

Ad preview

My great website
Best product ever
at the best price
www.mysite.com

Ad extensions expand your ad with additional inform
Take a tour

Keywords

⊟ Select keywords
Your ad can show on Google when people search for the keywords you choose here. These keywords will also automatically find relevant sites on keywords that relate directly to your ad. You can add more keywords later. Help me choose effective keywords.

Enter one keyword per line. Add keywords by spreadsheet

```
car cleaning products uk
interior car cleaning products
wholesale car cleaning products
professional car cleaning products
car cleaning products review
car cleaning products wholesale
cheap car cleaning products
```

▼ Category: Miscellaneous keywords
  « Add all from this category
  « Add   50megs member login
  « Add   free website service

[Re-estimate search traffic]

Estimated traffic summary ⑦
The following are approximations for the keywords above.
Based on max CPC: UK£2.72 and budget UK£10.00/day

Avg. CPC: £0.71 - £1.67

Clicks/day: 4 - 5

Cost/day: ⑦ UK£3.54 - UK£6.69

⊟ Advanced option: match types
  Use keyword match types to better target your ads:
  keyword = broad match
  "keyword" = match exact phrase
  [keyword] = match exact term only
  -keyword = don't match this term

Important note: We cannot guarantee that these keywords will improve your campaign performance. We reserve the right to disapprove any keywords you add. You are re the keywords does not violate any applicable laws.

Important

For ad quality reasons, it's very important that all the keywords within an ad group are very similar. To demonstrate exactly how similar they should be, here is an example list of keywords for a 'car cleaning products' keyword group:

- car cleaning products
- best car cleaning products
- waterless car cleaning products
- car cleaning products uk
- interior car cleaning products
- wholesale car cleaning products
- professional car cleaning products
- car cleaning products review
- car cleaning products wholesale
- cheap car cleaning products

As you can see, the variations are very slight.

4

Ad group default bids (Max. CPC)

You can influence your ad's position by setting its maximum cost-per-click (CPC) bid. This bid is the highest price you're willing to pay when someone clicks can change your bid as often as you like. Try a bid now to get started, then revise it later based on how your ads perform.

Default bid ⑦   UK£ 0.60

Display Network bid   UK£ 0.60
Leave blank to use automated bids. ⑦

Managed placements bid   UK£ 0.65
Optional: only necessary when adding managed placements ⑦

Save ad group   Cancel new ad group

4 Next, set up your maximum bid. For some reason, Google always recommends a very *high* maximum bid, but, in my experience, you don't need to bid that much to rank well. I therefore recommend setting your maximum bid at about 50 per cent of what Google suggests. When it comes down to it, what really matters is the click-through rate on the ad and the relevancy of your landing page, not how much you pay.

4

Creating your ad group (cont.)

5 Now all you have to do is review your selections and activate your account. Congratulations – you have set up your very first Google ad group.

For your information

When people ask what the best tips are for PPC, they assume the answer is some tool for bid management, trick in writing ads, or must have for landing page optimisation. The best tip however is a simple one: Organise your ad groups and campaigns like your business depends on it, because it does.

Tools, tricks and 'must haves' are just aides in the daily activities of a search marketer, paid or natural. They can reduce the amount of time you spend doing repetitive tasks, but they can't do it for you.

As with most advice when it comes to Internet marketing, there is no best way to organise ad groups and campaigns. It is going to depend on your business and goals. Just as each fingerprint is unique, each business is unique.

Organise your keywords according to products, geography or any other categorisation which is suitable for your business.

Search engine marketing (SEM) has two meanings. Which one comes into effect will depend on the way you use it. First, used purely as a means of publicity and an additional means of promotion, SEM requires the use of all the additional, paid-for techniques of gaining visibility online, which we have covered up to this point.

As part of normal SEO practice, however, SEM takes on its second, different meaning – namely, that of marketing the content you place on your site to search engines so they can index it better and start to list your site higher in their search engine results pages.

This is where complex SEO theory gives way to very practical actions. Your first step – before you

decide whether your site needs to be marketed to the search engine indices or not – needs to be to check to see the number of pages from your site that they each hold in their indexes.

Here's how this is done for the top three. Go to each search engine's website and type in the query box: **site:http://mysitedomain.co.uk**, substituting your website's domain name for the 'mysitedomain.co.uk' part. The result you get from each search engine will tell you just how many of your website's pages have been indexed and are on record in that search engine's index and, therefore, available to people making search queries.

How to get your website indexed by Google in less than 12 hours

You have a brand new website. Your website designers have optimised all your meta tags and you have put in all the relevant content. You are ready to do business and all you need now is to be found by the major search engines, including Google – fast!

You have paid for a website search engine submission service and now you are waiting. This is the hard part. Search engine submission services place your site on a database of sites to be indexed by search engines. Two developments have made this database incredibly large. First, new sites join the Web each day at the rate of over 200,000. Second, effective search engine submission services have become free, which means that they are used frequently and, therefore, a backlog has built up.

In practical terms, this means that your brand new site may remain invisible to search engines – and, therefore, to your potential online customers – for anything between six and eight weeks, in the best case, and six months, in the worst. What's more, different search engines have different response times for indexing sites from their database of sites to be indexed. Google has, usually, the fastest, at about six weeks, and MSN the slowest, at about three to five months. Google, of late, has also begun to respond slowly to indexing requests as the number of websites waiting to be indexed has grown.

At this point, you could be forgiven for feeling a little despair. After all, if your new website represents a significant investment in terms of money, time and effort, waiting to be found is the last thing you want.

Luckily for you, there is a solution that will allow for your website to be indexed within hours rather than weeks or months. Here's what you do:

If you have not already done so, go to **http://localsubmit.com/ free.asp** and have your website submitted to the top 40 search engines. Do not pay for the service and do not worry about submitting to any search engine outside the top 40 (even the top three – Google, Yahoo! and MSN – would do as these three publish feeds that then power hundreds of minor search engines on the Web). The reason you submit your site is so that you have gone through the process of alerting search engines it is there and waiting to be indexed.

1. Get the URL of your homepage and the URL of at least two other pages on your site that have some significant content in terms of providing value (which means they do not just list products) and go to the following social tagging sites:

   - **Digg** (http://digg.com) create an account there if you have not already got one, then copy and paste the URL and go through the process of submitting the three pages of your site that you have picked

   - **Delicious** (www.delicious. com) follow the same process there

   - **Newsvine** (www.newsvine. com) repeat as above.

2. Within five hours of having completed this exercise, the pages you have submitted will appear on the Google index.

What to do if your site has not been indexed properly

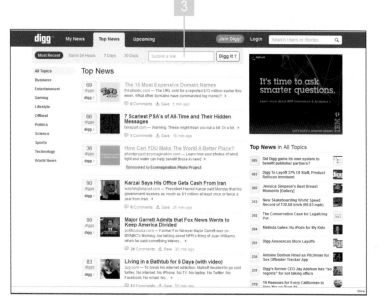

If your search engine index check returns a large number of pages which is close to the number of pages already on your site, that is good. If, however, there is a disparity, you need to take corrective action. Just follow the steps given.

1 Create an account at each of the following websites:

- http://digg.com

- www.orkut.com

- www.stumbleupon.com

- www.reddit.com

2 Create a list of your website's pages, with the URL of each one, a brief, two-line description and a set of keywords that best describe the content on that page. Start with the freshest content you have and work backwards from that.

3 Go to each of the accounts you created in step 1 and submit your site's content, using the URL, description and (when applicable) the keywords. Be careful! Submit only one page of your website at a time. Then go to the next one and so on. Finally, go to the first one and submit the next page. By spacing them out this way, you avoid setting off spam submission alarms. Within three days your site will have been indexed properly.

Anyone who was around at the turn of the century will remember the great Y2K fiasco as everyone worried that the so-called 'Millennium Bug' might crash the world's computers and usher us into the stone age as computer clocks updated. The point is that, with computers, nothing is fixed until it absolutely has to be and what started out remains with us until then. That is exactly the case with www and non-www domain names. You and I both know that **www.mysitename.co.uk** is exactly the same as **http://mysitename.co.uk** – they are the same website accessed via two routes so to speak. To a computer, though, and to a search engine, the two versions appear as different websites, which means that they also consider them to be two separate domain names.

One of the rules for SEO is how to address this issue as it causes a number of problems, in terms of how a search engine sees your website. What concerns us here is to find out which of the versions is best indexed in a search engine index and go with that as your main domain name. In order to do this, make sure that, when you query each search engine index, you use the traditional **www.domainname** format and then, the **http://domainname** format. The one that is indexed best will deliver the highest number of pages in the index of the search engine you are querying.

Domain name indexing – www versus http://

Timesaver tip

When it comes to domain name indexing you will have to make a decision about which one to promote. These days the emphasis is on convenience, speed and memorability so adding 'www.' in front of promotional text, ads or any promotional literature which has to do with your website is superfluous.

A simple HYPERLINK "http://yourdomainname.com" http://yourdomainname. com will suffice. Many print adverts today and quite a few television or radio ones do not even go that far. They simply state yourdomainname.com and that's it. They trust the end-user to remember to add www. or http://. This also makes it easier for you to choose which version of your website to promote.

4

SEO and website design

5

Introduction

The design of your website has an immediate impact on the way it is indexed and how it is weighed by search engines. In this chapter, you will see what the different elements of website design contribute to a website's SEO status. Also, what you can do to make sure your website design is not an obstacle to it being found by search engines.

What you'll do

Learn why website design can affect SEO

Learn about what search engine bots see on your website

See how to analyse a website's design

Find out what to do if your site structure is deeper than two layers

Learn how to find out if your website has been indexed

See how to market your content to search engines – create a sitemap

Learn how to build a trustworthy website

Find out how to optimise your website on a daily basis

Why website design can affect SEO ▶

In an ideal world, a website would be indexed, categorised and then served to anyone who happens to be looking for its content on an almost automatic basis. The world is far from ideal, however, so this simply does not happen, though, to be fair, when the Web was first conceived, the intention was for it to work in exactly that way.

The reason it does not happen has to do with inefficiency and lack of communication. For a medium that is supposed to thrive on both, the Web is a tangle of competing and sometimes conflicting standards. Server development, website-building languages and browser technology develop at different rates, for different reasons and in different directions.

The very lack of hierarchy that makes the Web so appealing, democratic and empowering works against you when it comes to your website and how well it will be indexed by the search engines you rely on to make it visible. Here are some website design problems that can adversely affect your website's SEO:

- sites with a vertical structure that buries old content as new items are posted on them

- Javascript, which links pages and is hard to follow for search engine bots

- links that go deep into the site in a link chain that is not always followed by search engine bots

- menu items that are either in Flash or clickable images and are essentially invisible to search engines.

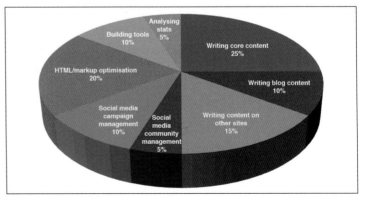

The percentages of SEO work required for a brand new website.

Search engines are, for the most part, websites run by a database that relies on automated software agents called spiders, crawlers, robots and bots. The bots seek content on the Web and play a key role in how search engines operate.

To be able to index the Internet, all search engines need a tool that is able to visit websites, navigate them, discern information about them, decide what the website is about and add that data to its index. This tool also has to be able to follow leads or links from one website to the next, so that it can continue to gather information and learn about the Internet indefinitely. If it does its job properly, then the search engine has a good, valuable database or index and will deliver relevant results to visitors' queries.

Unfortunately, the tools that the search engines depend on to add content to their databases are neither cutting edge, nor incredibly powerful. Search engine robots have very limited functionality, similar in power to that of early Web browsers in terms of what they can understand on a Web page. From the information that is visible to them, these spiders grab information such as page titles, meta tags, meta data and textual content to be included in the search engine's index or database.

If you would like to get an idea of what search engines see on a website, get your hands on a Version 3 Internet Explorer or Netscape Navigator browser. It's not always pretty, but, just like the early browsers, the search engine bots just don't know how to do certain things. These bots don't understand frames, Flash movies, images or JavaScript. They can't click any buttons on a website, so, if there isn't a static link for them to follow, they won't follow it. They can't navigate dropdown menus and can't run a search on your website to find the content. They also will probably be stopped in their tracks when attempting to index a dynamically generated website or one that uses JavaScript navigation.

What search engine bots see on your website

Jargon buster

Bot – Short for *robot*. These are web applications that can run the same task over and over again without needing supervision. Spiders are a type of bot, as are most junk emailing systems.

Spider – The software that crawls your site to try and determine the content it finds.

5

SEO and website design 75

What search engine bots see on your website (cont.)

One classic example of a site that is hard for a search engine to index because of its design is the English in a Box website (**http://englishinabox.com**). Human visitors see the site like this.

The creator of the website believed he had a visual guide that was intuitive and easy to navigate for people. What the Google bot sees, however, when it goes to this website is this.

```
<html xmlns="http://www.w3.org/1999/xhtml" xml:lang="en-gb" lang="en-gb">
<head>

  <base href="http://englishinabox.com/" />
  <meta http-equiv="content-type" content="text/html; charset=utf-8" />
  <meta name="robots" content="index, follow" />
  <meta name="keywords" content="English In a Box" />
  <meta name="description" content="English In a Box" />
  <meta name="generator" content="Joomla! 1.5 - Open Source Content Management" />
  <title>English In a Box</title>
  <link href="/index.php?format=feed&amp;type=rss" rel="alternate" type="application/rss+xml" title="RSS 2.0" />
  <link href="/index.php?format=feed&amp;type=atom" rel="alternate" type="application/atom+xml" title="Atom 1.0" />
  <link rel="stylesheet" href="http://englishinabox.com/templates/system/css/system.css" type="text/css" />
  <link rel="stylesheet" href="http://englishinabox.com/templates/system/css/general.css" type="text/css" />
  <link rel="stylesheet" href="http://englishinabox.com/templates/penguinmail/css/addons.css" type="text/css" />
  <link rel="stylesheet" href="http://englishinabox.com/templates/penguinmail/css/layout.css" type="text/css" />
  <link rel="stylesheet" href="http://englishinabox.com/templates/penguinmail/css/template.css" type="text/css" />
  <link rel="stylesheet" href="http://englishinabox.com/templates/penguinmail/css/joomla.css" type="text/css" />
  <link rel="stylesheet" href="http://englishinabox.com/templates/penguinmail/css/gk_stuff.css" type="text/css" />
  <link rel="stylesheet" href="http://englishinabox.com/templates/penguinmail/css/typo.css" type="text/css" />
  <link rel="stylesheet" href="http://englishinabox.com/templates/penguinmail/css/css3_style1.css" type="text/css" />
  <script type="text/javascript" src="/media/system/js/mootools.js"></script>
  <script type="text/javascript" src="http://englishinabox.com/templates/penguinmail/js/domready_fix.js"></script>
  <script type="text/javascript" src="/media/system/js/caption.js"></script>
  <script type="text/javascript" src="http://englishinabox.com/templates/penguinmail/js/gk.script.js"></script>

<!--[if IE 8.0]><link rel="stylesheet" href="http://englishinabox.com/templates/penguinmail/css/ie8.css" type="text/css" /><![endif]-->
<!--[if IE 7.0]><link rel="stylesheet" href="http://englishinabox.com/templates/penguinmail/css/ie.css" type="text/css" /><![endif]-->
<!--[if IE 7.0]><style>.clearfix { display: inline-block; } /* IE7xhtml*/</style><![endif]-->

<script type="text/javascript">
var siteurl='http://englishinabox.com/';
var tmplurl='http://englishinabox.com/templates/penguinmail';
</script>

<link href="http://englishinabox.com/templates/penguinmail/css/menu/mega.css" rel="stylesheet" type="text/css" /><script src="http://englishinabo
<link href="http://englishinabox.com/templates/penguinmail/fonts/PT-Seans/stylesheet.css" rel="stylesheet" type="text/css" />
<style type="text/css">
```

The website relies on purely visual appeal to the human visitor. As a result the search engine bot sees very little which can help it navigate or index the website properly, which means it won't be indexed and it will not get the traffic it needs.

When it comes to your website's design, you really need to know how to make it work so that it is search engine-friendly (SEF) and achieves a good position on the major search engines.

To do this it should:

- use intelligible links between pages
- never be made in Flash
- never be made up of images, because they cause many of the same issues as exist when using only Flash (mainly search engines cannot see them so they think that there is no content)
- have a nice easy-to-use navigation system that can be understood at a glance.

The first step to take when analysing your website for search engine-friendliness is to take a look at its visual layout. If 80 to 90 per cent of your website's content is within a two-tiered layer – that is, the most your human visitors will need to click in order to get to it is twice – then you are going in the right direction.

The screenshot is a good example of a homepage. Visitors need to only click twice to get to most of the content. This means that the site has a relatively flat structure so when you do land on the homepage you can get to most of what the site has to offer within two clicks.

How to analyse a website's design

Jargon buster

Flash – animation software that jazzes up websites. Search engines can't read it very well, so if your website is in flash you need to make sure you describe what's in it in HTML too so that you get indexed properly.

See also

See Chapter 2: Creating a search engine-friendly site.

5

What to do if your site structure is deeper than two layers

Redesigning a website is always expensive, but it is particularly annoying if it is already established and then you find that you have to pay out more to get its layout changed.

Luckily, there is a solution to this problem that is less radical than a total redesign and can be just as effective. The overriding need here is to help search engine bots follow the links on your website and index deeper content. This means you really need to bring that deeper content to the surface of the homepage.

One option is to implement a tag cloud on your website. This is a piece of automatic programming that indexes your website's content and creates a text box of the keywords. All of these are linkable to the content they came from and the most frequently used ones appear bigger within the tag cloud.

The other choice you have is to place at the bottom of your website text links leading to the deeper content on your website.

It is a good practice to organise your site like this anyway, but having it as an additional measure on a website that is suffering from content not being indexed properly (you know this has happened when your website's pages do not show up on search engines when you specifically look for them), it is a true lifesaver.

If your website is not search engine-friendly, you really need to know about it. The first indication is when you have a number of pages on your website but few of them actually appear on the search engines' indexes. Here's how to check this.

How to find out if your website has been indexed

1. Go to Google, Yahoo! and Bing and type the following command in the search engine field: **site:http://www. mywebsite.com** (replacing the words 'mywebsite' with your own domain name).

2. Look at the number of pages of your site which are reported as being present in the search results.

3. If the number of pages in the Google Index is higher than the total number of pages on your website do not worry, there are technical reasons for this.

4. If the number of pages on the Google Index is *lower* than the total number of pages on your website then you need to take direct action, including changing the structure of your website to fix this or implementing the additions covered earlier in this chapter (tag cloud, flat website structure, text links at the bottom of the website). You also need to create a sitemap.

5

How to market your content to search engines – create a sitemap

▶

In order to overcome the issue of different numbers of pages being indexed, you need to market your content to search engines so that their bots visit your site and start serving your pages. There are a few steps you need to take to achieve this, beginning with the creation of an XML sitemap.

Luckily there is an easy way to create a sitemap now.

1 Go to: **www.auditmypc.com/ free-sitemap-generator.asp** and click the **Sitemap generator** icon there.

2 Accept all the choices it asks you to make, including a security certificate, to be taken to the next screen.

3 Make sure that you have input your domain name in the URL box and ticked the box asking that your website be indexed from anywhere.

Jargon buster

Sitemap – An XML file that lists all the URLs for a website. The XML sitemap file enables a webmaster to inform search engines about URLs on a website that are available for crawling so they are included on the search engine's database. It is, essentially, a roadmap for the content on your website.

1

3

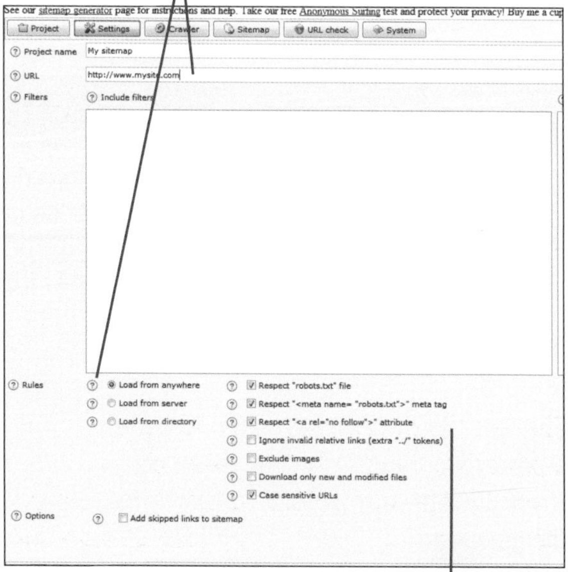

2

4 **5**

See our sitemap generator page for instructions and help. Take our free Anonymous Surfing test and protect your privacy! Buy me a c

6

7

That's it! You've done it! You now have given search engines a powerful roadmap to your website's structure and content. If you update your website regularly, you will need to repeat the generation of your sitemap each time so that it is always up to date.

How to market your content to search engines – create a sitemap (cont.)

4 Click the green **Play** button at the bottom of the screen. Indexing your website will take some time, so be patient. You will be able to see the pages accumulating as their URLs are being collected.

5 Once the indexing process has been completed and the sitemap is ready, go to the top of the screen and click **Sitemap**.

6 Next, choose **Export** and export the sitemap in XML format.

7 Make a note of where it has been saved in your computer or laptop, then go there, right-click on the file and make sure that its name is 'sitemap'. When you have renamed it, you should have a file labelled sitemap.xml.

8 Use an FTP client like the one you use to currently update your website and upload your sitemap to the root directory of your website.

5

How to build a trustworthy website

The entire point of SEO work is that your website begins to appear naturally on the search engine organic results page. Why? Because independent research by Comcast and Netpoint has shown that searchers tend to trust websites that appear high on the organic search engine page results more than those in the online ads results column, so click on them and do business with them more than the online ads ones. This means that if your website is not also optimised to capitalise on the visitors you get, you are missing a real opportunity to make a sale.

So, how exactly do you convert online visitors into online customers? Here are four basic tips to help you do just that.

- **Show your visitors who you are** If you are asking people to send you money for a service or product, make sure they know who you are, that you are a person they understand, what your motivation is and why you have set up this site.

- **Show your visitors that you're different** Unless you happen to sell a product or service that no one else has thought of before, the chances are that you have competitors. Your online visitors should know exactly how you are different from all your competitors.

- **Show your awards and testimonials from satisfied customers** Online visitors, like each of us, are swayed by other people's opinions. Display testimonials and show what your clients think and you are halfway to overcoming most objections. Similarly, if you have won awards or comply with some particular industry standard or industry compliance requirement, show it in order to prove that you are a serious business.

- **Show your terms and conditions regarding doing business with you** This is an expansion on the engendering trust in an online transaction. Make sure your online visitors can easily access your T & Cs, guarantees and anything else governing doing business with you.

Plus, of course, make sure you have optimised your website in terms of SEO elements so that it shows up high on the organic search engine results page.

For nearly every website, there is a lot of online competition. This makes optimising your website harder – not just because there are many things to do but also because the fact that your website has competitors selling a similar product or service makes it more difficult to convince Google your site is not a spam site. This is a task that gets harder the more online competition you face.

If you are selling products or services online, the chances are that your competitors are selling similar products or services with very similar descriptions. No matter how original you try to be with your descriptions, there is only a finite number of ways you can describe a product or a service and still make sense. Things become even harder if you have to include technical information and product specifications.

Because of such similarities in content, Google looks at new sites that optimise their content consistently and aggressively with a certain degree of scepticism. Red flags do not exactly go up, but the site will not be indexed fast nor served high on the Google search page results.

You should check that your website is being 'tested' by Google on a daily basis, as shown in Steps 1–5. If it is you will see that, in the first couple of months, a relatively low number of pages will have been indexed and the figure will vary from day to day.

If this is happening to your site, the advice you are about to receive will let you get past this. Google is being naturally cautious because the number of spam sites that come online each year is truly staggering. It really wants to make sure your site is a bona fide one and has something of value to offer.

The first thing you need to do is, in the beginning, hold back a little. If, for instance, you were about to drop 5000 words of content in a day, you would be better advised to stagger it, dropping a little each day rather than all at once.

In terms of gaining Google's confidence and acceptance, 'nice and easy' is very much the approach. Any sudden spikes of activity will raise red flags for Google. The same thing goes

How to optimise your website on a daily basis

How to tell if your website is being tested by Google

1 Go to **Google.co.uk** (or **Google.com** if you are testing the search engine's US Index).

2 In the search field type the query: **site:http://mysitename.com** (replace the words 'mysitename' with the name of your site).

3 Make a note of the result which will be displayed. It will be an xxx number of pages.

4 Perform the same search the next day. Again, make a note of the pages shown by the search engine.

5 Variations in the number of pages in the Google Index indicate that the site is still under review and pages are being picked up and dropped. The site will stabilise after a while and that's when it begins to become trusted by Google.

5

How to optimise your website on a daily basis (cont.)

for your link building. Suddenly putting together 600 links in a week is bound to cause your new site to be noticed for all the *wrong* reasons. Instead, tabulate your time and build links on a steady, daily basis.

Optimise your website in this way and you will soon see that the number of pages being indexed begins to rise and remain steady, building on a gradual basis. This is clear-cut evidence that your site is being indexed properly and will start to appear higher on search engine results pages than at the start.

Timesaver tip

When you work online time is always against you. I use my browser to give me some SEO shortcuts which I will share with you. To achieve this you must be using Firefox (**http://www.mozilla.com/en-US/firefox/**). When you have it installed add these three tools:

1 Track Me Not (**http://www.seobook.com/**). This is a very helpful add-on. You might have noticed that your website will eventually come up first when searching for it every day in Google. Track Me Not helps you see the real progress of your website no matter how many times you search for it every day. It basically hides your search trails in a 'cloud' of different popular queries, and that way you are able to really see how your website is doing.

2 Similar Web (**https://addons.mozilla.org/en-US/firefox/ addon/similarweb-sites-recommendation/**). This add-on helps you find similar websites to the one you are currently on. Similar Web is very helpful when you need to find other websites with the similar purpose (like Directories, for instance).

3 NoDoFollow (**https://addons.mozilla.org/en-US/firefox/ addon/nodofollow/**). Click on Options new and then the ad-on. Then just click on it and it will highlight all the links on the web page you are looking at. The NoFollow links will be highlighted in red and the DoFollow ones in blue.

SEO and product promotion

Introduction

SEO becomes vital when marketing goods, products or services online is required. This is, after all, one of the main areas in which it is most frequently applied and there is always pressure, the moment you set up a commercial website, to make it as visible as possible.

How to use product descriptions to benefit your SEO

▶

When you have a commercial website selling products, the scope for originality is, understandably, a little weak. This, does not mean, however, that you will be unable to use the process of describing what your website is selling to help your SEO and your website's standing with search engines. The checklist below is designed to help you do just that.

■ Don't use the manufacturer's descriptions for the products you're selling. If you search online for the first line of the description and see how many results there are, you'll discover that almost all of your competitors will be using the same product descriptions. You won't want to incur a duplicate content penalty, nor do you want to spend time and energy going toe-to-toe with everyone else. You understand what you are selling, so work out why you are selling it (what need does it meet?) and go from there.

■ Do not generalise what you are selling. Write your content for your *exact* target audience. If you're selling baby products, then you'll want to target new parents. If you're selling an exclusive apartment, then you'll be targeting young professionals. Encouraging people to invest in stocks and shares will be harder than persuading a family to add groceries to their online shopping basket.

■ You'll want to make sure that your content is suitable for the products you're selling. Selling a sports car will call for a different style of writing from that appropriate to selling a washing machine or children's clothes. Make sure that what you actually write does, indeed, sell.

■ Utilise your keywords, where possible and relevant, to help your SEO campaign. Your target audience might search for a model name or brand or what the product does, so you'll need to consider all these factors in your product titles and descriptions, including them everywhere possible.

■ Don't over use your keywords, though – it will make the copy hard to read and be obvious that you have tried to optimise your copy for the search engines. There is nothing more offputting for visitors than text that is hard to read because it is stuffed with keywords and an unnatural style of writing as these things really do not appeal.

- Use calls to action to encourage your visitors to become customers. 'Find out more about ...', 'Call us now to order', 'Add to basket', 'Costs less than a cup of coffee a day', 'Buy now to avoid disappointment', 'Reserve your copy now', 'Just three days left' – these are just some examples of phrases that can encourage sales. Again, think of *why* you would buy your product and go from there.

- Remember that you need to *explain* why people need your products. Nobody wants to buy a new TV when their existing TV works or spend £4000 on a family holiday when they can go to Spain for £300. Explain the benefits and emphasise certain points to show why they can't live without your product and why it is superior to its competitors.

- Use emotions and situations rather than just dry facts to describe your products. A dining table can become much more desirable if you mention that it is can be easily cleaned so it is suitable for young families and your visitors will be impressed with a lightweight sleeping bag that will fit in a rucksack, so is suitable for taking to music festivals. Remember, your product needs to solve an emotional need first and a practical one second.

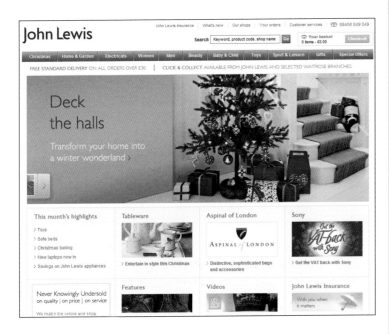

How to use product descriptions to benefit your SEO (cont.)

- Include dimensions, times and other details, if relevant, so that your visitors know how big or small your product is or how long it takes to work. Use comparisons, too, so that the measurements are easy to understand, such as 'slightly larger than a deck of cards', 'weighing less than a bag of sugar', 'small enough to fit in your pocket', 'takes less time to work than it does to make a cup of tea', 'in less time than it takes to boot up your computer'. These are credible ways to describe your product and give your visitors proper indications of how big or heavy your product is and how quick it is. Rather than saying that it's 10 cm long, and weighs 100 g, you can say that it's smaller and lighter than most chocolate bars – people will then know exactly what it's like.

- Include links to other relevant products or information in your description. Why not say that it's part of the 'ABCD range' or 'ideal for use with product ABC' and like them? The aim is to make it as easy as possible for your visitors to buy. It also showcases your expertise, that you really know what you are talking about and helps create additional sales, which are all good for your business.

When you have a commercial website it is important to keep relevant information coming into it on a regular basis. In order to succeed in this, you need to be aware of keywords, which means keyword density.

Keyword density, you will recall from Chapter 3, is the percentage of times a keyword or phrase appears on a Web page compared to the total number of words on the page. In the context of SEO, keyword density can be used as a factor for determining whether or not a Web page is relevant to a specified keyword or keyword phrase.

In the late 1990s – which were the early days of search engines – keyword density was an important factor in relation to how a page was ranked. As webmasters discovered this and the implementation of optimum keyword density became widespread, however, it became a minor factor in the rankings. Search engines began giving priority to other factors beyond the direct control of webmasters to avoid this happening. Thus, today, the overuse of keywords – a practice called keyword stuffing – will cause a Web page to be penalised.

The problem is that, even as you write for search engine indexing and search engine inclusion, you also need to keep an eye on making it suitable for human readers who will be brought to the site alongside the search engine bots.

The first question is what is it best to write and the second is how should it be written? What should you be aiming for and how do you do it and check afterwards? To illustrate, we will use the post below and the words we will aim to optimise for are 'SEO blog' and 'keyword density'. It makes sense, each time you do this, to have one primary keyword and one secondary.

Having an SEO blog is a great help because, unlike a more formal article, an SEO blog allows you to create entries that are almost chatty in style and have the correct keyword density without it feeling forced.

◄ **Keyword density, blogs and how to attract traffic to your website**

6

Timesaver tip

If you create content for your website directly online this Firefox add on will save you time. You need to have Firefox in order to run it. If you have not got it already, it can be downloaded from (**http://www.mozilla.com/en-US/firefox/**). Once you have it go to: **http://labs.wordtracker.com/seo-blogger/** and download and install the SEO Blogger Keyword Tool. The plugin puts this nifty little 'w' at the bottom right of your screen so you can click on it any time you want to instantly do some keyword research. It will save you a lot of time and effort.

Keyword density, SEO blogs and how to attract traffic to your website (cont.)

See also

To check the keyword density of the website text you are optimising, see Chapter 1.

Did you know?

Blog posts are a central part of a website's content creation strategy helping it to generate a large number of relevant keywords which in turn attracts visitors.

The theme of your SEO blog can be anything at all – something topical, a thought you had, an observation … These kinds of items make an SEO blog compelling and easy to read, as well as allowing you to use the right kinds of keywords to contribute to building the keyword density you require and the key to it is exactly its informality.

SEO blogs and blogs in general are indexed by search engines more regularly than normal Web pages. They allow for fast, constant updating of a website and provide links to other pages, which allows them to also be crawled by search engine bots.

The primary keyword you are looking to optimise your website for should have a keyword density of no more than 16 per cent, while the secondary one should have a keyword density of anywhere between 2 and 4 per cent.

As you can see, by choosing a primary keyword – *keyword density* – and a secondary one – *SEO blog* – I was able in this particular piece of writing to build up the keyword density in a way that provides the right compromise between material that has been optimised to be read by humans, and is therefore not so keyword density-driven, and material optimised to be read by search engine bots, so needs to have the right keyword density in order to help your website.

The question is, of course, just how do you choose the *right* keyword and how do you get the right *keyword density* on the page? The answer is that you pick a word which reflects your site's nature, thereby leading to thematic linking, so it builds, on a gradual basis, with all the rest of the stuff on your website, so the keyword density of one particular SEO blog entry is not out of sync with the entries coming after it or before it and the density of each contributes to marking your website out as an authority on a particular subject, such as SEO.

Keyword density, SEO blogs and how to attract traffic to your website (cont.)

6

!

Important

Keyword density is an important aspect of your SEO activity. Always choose a primary keyword and a secondary for each SEO blog entry you put together. Make sure that you check the keyword density so it is correct and pick the keywords to thematically link with the rest of the site.

The keyword density of your primary keyword *must be* no more than 5 per cent and that of your secondary keyword *no more* than 3 per cent. Try to be judicious about the use of your keywords so that the density is a carefully worked out balance between organic, natural writing and keyword density-driven text that is optimised for search engines.

?

Did you know?

77% of Internet users read blogs.

There are currently 133 million blogs listed on leading blog directory Technorati.

60% of bloggers are between the ages 18–44.

One in five bloggers update their blogs daily.

Two thirds of bloggers are male.

Corporate blogging accounts for 14% of blogs.

15% of bloggers spend 10 hours a week blogging.

More than 50% of bloggers have more than one blog.

Bloggers use an average of five different social sites to drive traffic to their blog.

Targeted optimisation: the secret of successful SEO

▶

In your drive to optimise your website for inclusion on Google's top pages, it is incredibly easy to become blinkered and lose sight of the wood for the trees.

We have just seen the importance of keywords. As a matter of fact, when you strip SEO activities from much of the technical stuff you have to do, what remains is content and keywords. Simple, right?

That's where many go wrong – very wrong. The temptation, for example, to optimise a website straight away for the name of the product it sells is so great that very few webmasters can resist it. Broadly speaking, it is not a bad thing to do, but, bearing in mind that time is money and creating content, waiting for it to be indexed and then waiting for an appraisal of the results in terms of traffic numbers and purchases made (which, after all is the clearest indication of the SEO success of your website and its ability to attract targeted visitors) all take time, by the time you have reached the point at which you begin to realise something is wrong with your SEO efforts, you have spent a heck of a lot of money.

So, straight to the point: what should you be doing, right from the start, to make sure your SEO efforts are exactly what they should be?

The trick here is to wear the right hat as you approach SEO. When you are creating your list of keywords that will guide your content creation and website optimisation efforts, do not just approach the project from the expert owner with in-depth product knowledge angle, but also look at your site and the way it sells its products and services from a purely customer or first-time visitor angle.

Here is an example that drives this point home. When we first launched HelpMySEO, within four days it made Google's top page for the search term 'Help My SEO' against over 14 million competing pages at the time. Had we been planning to optimise it for that search term (we had not), we would have been justified in popping some Champagne corks and organising for some catering people to throw a small party for us.

That, though, would have been incredibly shortsighted. For a start, 'Help My SEO' is a phrase that we would assume (quite correctly as it turns out) few people looking for tips or help for their sites would actually type into a search engine. Even worse, for a new webmaster, the term 'Help My SEO' is about as outlandish as typing 'newly minted webmaster independently seeks onpage optimisation tips for nascent website', which, I hope, perfectly illustrates the problem.

In order to be successful, we had to approach the search terms that would be typed into a search engine from a new user's point of view – somebody looking for tips and advice on how to optimise his or her website.

That is exactly what you should be doing for your website when creating your list of keywords. You need to think, 'If I was completely new to this, knew nothing about the business and was looking for a product or service my website sells, what would I type into the search engine, hoping to find it?'

Sometimes, you're lucky and the search terms that come up exactly describe the product or service you happen to sell on your website. In more cases than you would think, however, the search terms entered by *users* are not the same as the search terms *you* have been optimising your website for. It is in this that the problem lies.

The keywords you choose are the core of your SEO strategy. Most new webmasters fall at this first hurdle because they optimise their websites for keywords written from a webmaster point of view rather than an online visitor point of view.

How to laser-drill your keywords

1 Get pen and paper.

2 Write down all the keywords which your potential customers are most likely to use. Be careful that you do not slip jargon in there, or any words which you as the 'expert' know.

3 Once you have a list of a good dozen or so words, think of what questions your website visitors will be asking themselves when looking for your website.

4 Now write down the keywords associated with the answers to those questions.

5 You now have a list of keywords around which your website content can begin to revolve. This is the first step towards White Hat, long-term, quality SEO.

Using the power of the Web to generate phone sales ▶

1. Sign in to your Google AdWords account and use **Ad Extensions** to add your address and phone number.

2. In order to set up the click-to-call functionality for your site, you must first set up a location extension. This ensures that your customers are shown the phone number for your business location nearest to them when they find your listing on their phone or PDA.

3. Include your phone number. If you're using addresses from a Local Business Center account, you'll have to login to view or edit your listing.

4. Advertise on high-end mobiles. Make sure that you've opted in to showing your ads on iPhones and other mobile devices with full Internet browsers. Check which devices you are advertising on from the Settings tab for your AdWords campaign.

The Web is at its best when it allows us to leverage its global presence and benefit locally. In order for this to work the way it should, we need to be aware of the many different ways those who may be looking for our services or products are searching for us, then work hard to make it as easy as possible for them to access what we have to offer.

Easy as this may sound conceptually, in practice it is much harder to do because there are many different ways in which potential clients might find you and your efforts need to cover as many of them as possible if you are to be successful.

If research into online consumer behaviour shows anything at all, it is the fact that consumers tend to be opportunistic, using the types of searches most convenient to them and being unwilling to spend huge amounts of time looking for what you are selling. This puts the pressure on you, as a website owner, to make sure that they find you no matter how they may be searching for you.

That is where localisation and phone capability come in. With the world's mobile users outnumbering PC users by about two to one, Google has set its sights firmly on the mobile platform market. As a result, its AdWords now offers two ways to show click-to-call phone numbers on text ads that are shown to users with high-end mobile devices featuring full Internet browsers.

You can use location extensions to add your phone number so that it can be viewed and click-to-call access by customers who may be close to your business locations so that they can then click and call the moment they have found you. This may result in an instant order (the best case scenario) or a query, but, in either case, we have full engagement, which is the first step towards achieving sales.

There are four easy steps shown opposite to ensure that your business phone number is set up to enable users with iPhones and other smart mobile devices with full Internet browsers to click to call the number that appears at the end of your ad text.

Google has amalgamated the functionality of Google Places with the immediacy and analytics power of Google Local Business Center in order to help local business to get more customers through their doors free of charge. Use Google Places to create your free listing, and when potential customers search Maps for local information, they'll find your business – your address, opening hours, even photos of your shopfront or products. See the screenshots below for an example of the difference this can make: the old advertisement is placed over on the top right, the new placement is now more visible on the right and is framed by images.

To register for a free Google Places account go to the website (at: **www.google.com/places**). The process is intuitive and, once you have registered, fill in all the required fields and then simply wait for your listing to be verified.

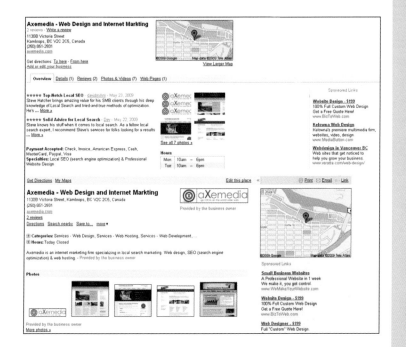

?

Did you know?

One of the most powerful ways to help your online business to be found by the community in which you trade is to register with Google Places. Formerly known as Google Local Business Center, Google Places gives you the power to drive local customers to your business without even having a website (though, obviously, having one gives you an added edge).

1 Sign in to your AdWords account at Google AdWords (at: **www.adwords.google.com**).

2 Click the campaign you want to edit.

3 Click the **Settings** tab.

How to add or edit a location extension in your ads (cont.)

4 Click on **Ad extensions** and then **Location extensions > Phone extensions**.

5 Choose a campaign and then click on **New extension**. Choose the campaign you have set up from your **Campaigns** panel (shown). From the drop down box below find the country you are in and then input your telephone number. Make sure you include area code but no country code. If your website is not set up or if your website is not mobile device compatible you will need to tick the Call-only format box. This makes sure that those who find your business on a mobile device can call you with just a click. If your website is mobile device compatible leave this box unchecked.

6 Click **Save**. That's it, you've done it.

The number of links that come into your site are important for many different reasons. They:

- bring in additional traffic
- help to improve your site's page ranking
- are powerful aids in terms of indexing your site.

It is almost as important to know how to link *from* your site as it is to know how to link *to* your site. Here we will examine practical strategies for both.

Links running *from* your site

Each time you have a link that leads *away* from your site, the golden rule to set it to open in a new window rather than the same window in which your site opens. The reason is simple. Every time you have a link leading away like this, you increase the likelihood that the person clicking it will not come back to your site – particularly if they click two or more times, getting further and further away with each click.

By having those links that lead away from you open in a new window, you ensure your site is still open and easy to see, even if the person becomes engrossed and clicks on dozens of other sites' pages.

A perfect example of this is in the screenshot below. There, the link in the article that leads to the RSPCA's website opens it up in an entirely separate window.

Internal linking strategies for your website (cont.)

See also

See 'Linking strategies that help your SEO' in Chapter 8.

Links leading to your sales page on your website

Again, here you need to be careful. Your sales page should be no more than one click deep from anywhere on your site. Anything that increases the number of steps a person has to take in order to purchase from you raises a perceptual barrier to them making a purchase.

Similarly, research has shown that the more options you give your customers at purchase level, the fewer sales you will actually make. Ensure that when they get to your sales page, they are there to buy or try or go back and that's it.

Links leading to other pages

Finally, make sure your site has the kind of navigation that creates a cross-spidered image – that is, each page links to as many other pages as possible, either via text links or dynamic navigation buttons. This is a useful tactic for raising the internal PageRank for pages on your site as well as a tactic employed to help spread the PageRank for your homepage to internal pages within your site.

Here is a problem every website owner comes up against. You've just dropped new content onto your site. You expect to see results fast and you want the new content to be indexed because it may be topical. What do you do?

One thing you should *not* do is leave it to the mercy of the search engine bot schedule – particularly if the content is topical, such as a Christmas promotion or a product that relates to a specific news event.

The fast way round this problem is to give search engine bots plenty of other ways to find your site and the particular content you dropped in. The fastest way to do this is give the content a social tag.

Social tagging is the result of specific networks where you can promote your site's content so that it can be found and perhaps promoted by the network's users. This may lead to a little more traffic for your website, but that is not our main focus here. Social networks are search engine bot magnets. Because their content changes so fast, they are indexed very hour. We want to take advantage of this constant indexing to short-circuit the process to our benefit.

So, how do we achieve this? Well, first, join some of the major social tagging networks. Some of the best to join are Digg (**http://digg.com**), StumbleUpon (**www.stumbleupon.com**) and Delicious (**www.delicious.com**).

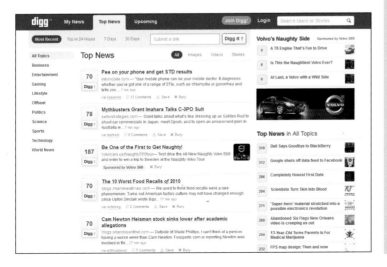

Social tagging: your shortcut to fast indexing (cont.)

Registration takes only minutes and the moment after you register you can begin to promote your website's content.

Two things happen when you register on these networks and promote your content with a link to your website:

- Provided your site's content is unique and has as much value as you can possibly throw at it, you may find it being promoted by the network's members, who pass it to each other and friends, which leads to traffic for your website.

- Search engine bots follow the links from the social tagging networks back to your website, which results in faster indexing as they are more likely to encounter your site's content as it spreads across a social tagging network than otherwise.

It's all about participation or people. The more visible you are on a site, the more likely you are to be voted for. Comment, submit stories, join in discussions about the community. People often act on impulse, so, if they recognise you as someone who submits great content, then they will be much more likely to vote your stories up. Remember, this also works the other way round, so behave!

Understand that it's work. The Jack of all trades is master of none, so unless you have an obscene amount of time to devote to profile building, don't try to become 'front page worthy' on all the social tagging sites out there. Instead, expect to spend 30 minutes to an hour a day on any of the sites you want to become a 'power user' on. It's much better to build an extremely strong profile on a small number of sites than have dozens of weak, useless ones. Find the niche that is most valuable for your type of content and build into it.

It all comes back to sweat. If you want to do well in social tagging, you need to figure out whether it's worth the time or not. There are dozens and dozens of ways to build traffic and social tagging is only one of them. Weigh up your options carefully and see which way is right for your business.

Social tagging: your shortcut to fast indexing (cont.)

6

Creating social tagging accounts

Go to each of the social tagging websites listed here and create an account for yourself.

1 http://digg.com

2 www.stumbleupon.com

3 www.delicious.com

4 www.orkut.com

5 www.reddit.com

6 www.newsvine.com

7 www.google.com/buzz

8 www.buzz.yahoo.com

SEO and online marketing

7

Introduction

SEO is important because it enables us, as webmasters, to increase traffic and, therefore, sales from our websites. What initially started out as a very technical aspect of website promotion has, over the last few years, evolved into activities that converge with online marketing.

In this chapter, we shall see what online marketing is, as opposed to SEO, and where the two reach common ground. The intent is to help you identify those areas in which your SEO and online marketing efforts can become one and the same, helping you to save time and effort.

You will also learn how to make your SEO work in sync with your online marketing, how to make your online marketing help your SEO, how to market effectively to search engines and how to gauge the effectiveness of any social media campaign you put in place.

What you'll do

Find out what online marketing is

Learn about SEO and online marketing – differences and similarities

Find out which social media and social tagging sites your website should have a presence on

Discover the benefits of social networking

Learn about SEO and directories

See how your site will be appropriate for various niche directories

Online marketing – what it is

The interactive nature of online marketing – in terms of providing instant responses and eliciting responses – is the unique quality of the medium. Online marketing is sometimes considered to be broad in scope because it not only refers to marketing on the Internet but also includes marketing via e-mail and wireless media. Management of digital customer data and electronic customer relationship management (ECRM) systems are also often grouped together under the term online marketing.

Online marketing ties together creative and technical aspects of the Internet, including design, development, advertising and sales.

Online marketing also refers to the placement of media at many different stages of the customer engagement cycle via search engine marketing (SEM), SEO banner ads on specific websites, e-mail marketing and Web 2.0 strategies.

Essentially, online marketing is an ever-expanding group of activities designed to increase awareness of your online presence by both search engines and the online population.

Let's begin first with some basics. In order to successfully market your website today, you need to leverage the popularity of social media networks.

The term 'social networks' describes websites that allow users to share content, media, news and information. Common examples are the popular social networking sites, such as Friendster, Facebook, MySpace, YouTube, Photobucket and Flickr (there are hundreds more). Social media are not restricted to the sharing of text data but also include video and photographs. Some networks specialise in the sharing of news and online reference sources, examples of which are Digg and Wikipedia, which are also counted in the social media bucket. Micro-blogging sites such as Twitter can also be included as social media.

Before we even see what you should be doing in online marketing and social networks, it is worth exploring in detail why social network marketing helps your SEO. Modern search engine algorithms use a large number of metrics designed to help them ascertain just how important a website is. Some of this we shall see in Chapter 9 when we discuss the importance of the social Web, but, for now, it is enough to understand that the appearance of your website's name and URL in social networks is a plus in the eyes of search engines, which then use it as a means of judging your website's importance in their listings.

?

Did you know?

■ **News Corporation (NWS)** owns Myspace, the second most viewed website in the world. It also purchased Photobucket, a photo-sharing website.

■ **Yahoo! (YHOO)** has been making moves to enter the social media segment. Its Flickr photo-sharing website and 360 social networking site are examples of this.

■ **Google (GOOG)** purchased YouTube, a leading online video-sharing website.

■ **Microsoft (MSFT)** announced a minority $240 million investment in Facebook in late October, valuing the company at an estimated $5 to $15 billion overall.

SEO and online marketing – differences and similarities (cont.)

The difference between SEO and online marketing lies in the fact that, when you are focused on marketing online, exclusively to human visitors, you employ channels of communication and means of communication that are focused more on users' needs than keywords and brand names. You would also be more likely to use media-rich marketing, such as photographs and video – both of which search engines cannot read.

When you market your website so that search engines will see it (and you might also get some human visitors), your focus is more on text-driven items that have links leading directly back to your website.

As you might imagine, this is an area that is being constantly refined, with the differences between the two activities becoming fewer and the similarities growing. That is why the metrics used to gauge the effectiveness of a social media campaign intended to help your online business reputation grow and one where you are looking for search engine marketing success are identical. Let's see what they are.

- **Traffic** Under the 'traffic' umbrella there are multiple metrics that are equally important when analysing success – page views for the campaign for one. It is pretty obvious, but it all starts with how much traffic the specific page generates throughout its 'viral' lifespan, as well as each month afterwards.

- **Unique visitors** Equally as obvious is the correlation between *total* visits and *unique* visits. This enables you to see what kind of new reach you have gained as a result of a campaign you have put in place.

- **Referring URLs** This is by far one of the most important metrics to track and watch. Knowing which social sites send you the most traffic and which blogs and news hubs are picking you up is very valuable. This helps you to manage the entire conversation, the influence the sites have in your niche and which of the sites sending you traffic is sending visitors who are engaging in your content. Understanding the referring sites that send you the best traffic will help you in your future campaigns.

Conversions Not all campaigns generate direct sales or leads from the initial burst in traffic and referrals, but, if your content does, make sure that you are tracking where they have come from. Some sites receive more leads from StumbleUpon (**www.stumbleupon.com**), whereas other sites get their leads from Digg (**http://digg.com**), Twitter (**http://twitter.com**) or Mashable (**http://mashable.com**). When companies start out in viral marketing, a lot of it can be shoot first and aim later, but as you better understand your conversions, you can be more targeted in the approach you take.

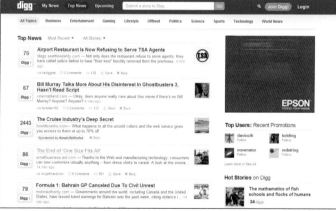

Micro-conversions Social media can build on small successes. You may not generate leads after your first influx in traffic, you may not sell crates full of your products, but you can build a large audience, so it is essential that you are tracking this. Use your Google Analytics to find out exactly where your clicks are coming from as explained in the steps.

1 Visit **https://www.google.com/ analytics/**. Click on **Access Analytics** and log in using your Google account.

2 You'll be prompted to sign up for Google Analytics. Click the **Sign Up** button.

3 To start the account sign up process you'll be prompted to enter your website's domain name, your site's country and time zone. Google will automatically create an account name for you based on your domain name, but you can override it if you have a preference. Click the **Continue** button.

4 After agreeing to Google's T&Cs, you've arrived at the tracking code. Google offers both the 'new' and 'legacy' tracking code. I can't imagine why you'd want to go with the legacy tracking code, so select and copy the new tracking code.

5 This code goes on the bottom of every Web page you want to track just before the `</body>` tag. You'll either want to add it yourself or share it with your Web developer.

Social media and social tagging sites your website should have a presence on ▶

Each of the social network and social bookmarking websites mentioned below is one your company or personal business website should have a presence on.

- **Reddit** (**www.reddit.com**) Upload stories and articles on reddit to drive traffic to your site or blog. Submit items often so that you'll gain a loyal following and increase your presence on the site.

- **Digg** (**http://digg.com**) Digg has a huge following online because of its optimum usability. Visitors can submit and browse articles in categories such as technology, business, entertainment, sports and more.

- **Delicious** (**www.delicious.com**) Social bookmark your way to better business with sites such as this one, which invite users to organise and publicise interesting items by tagging them and networking.

- **StumbleUpon** (**www.stumbleupon.com**) You'll open your online presence up to a whole new audience by just adding the StumbleUpon toolbar to your browser and then you can 'channel surf the Web'. You'll 'connect with friends and share your discoveries', as well as 'meet people that have similar interests'.

- **Ning** (**www.ning.com**) After hanging around the same social networks for a while, you may feel inspired to create your own, where you can bring together clients, vendors, customers and co-workers in a confidential, secure corner of the Web. Ning lets users design free social networks that they can share with anyone.

- **Squidoo** (**www.squidoo.com**): According to Squidoo, 'everyone's an expert on something. Share your knowledge!' Share your industry's secrets by answering questions and designing a profile page to help other members.

- **Diigo** (**www.diigo.com**): Make Diigo 'your personal Web file' by bookmarking great sites and sharing them with other users, recommending links, commenting on articles and utilising other fantastic features.

- **YouTube** (**www.youtube.com**) Everyone has a video floating around on YouTube. Shoot a behind-the-scenes video for your company's latest commercial or event to give customers and clients an idea of what you do each day.

Timesaver tip

Clever browsing technology allows you to make social sharing easier for Firefox or Chrome. If you do not have Firefox it can be downloaded at: **http://www.mozilla.com/en-US/firefox/**. Chrome can be downloaded at: **http://www.google.com/chrome**.

Once you have either browser set up go to Shareholic at: **http://www.shareaholic.com/** and download the add on. Once it's installed on your browser you will be able with just one click to publicise any content you want on the social networks straight from your browser. You will need, of course, to have an account on each one.

Shareaholic features over 300 social network tagging services and you get to choose which ones you want to use.

- **Ecademy (www.ecademy.com)** Ecademy prides itself on 'connecting business people' by means of its online network, blog and message board chats, as well as its premier BlackStar membership programme, which awards exclusive benefits.

- **Xing (www.xing.com)** An account with networking site Xing can 'open doors to thousands of companies'. Use the professional contact manager to organise your new friends and colleagues and take advantage of the Business Accelerator application to 'find experts at the click of a button, market yourself in a professional context [and] open up new sales channels'.

- **Facebook (www.facebook.com)** is the largest social network on the planet. Businesses vie for advertising opportunities, event promotion and more on this social networking site.

Social media and social tagging sites your website should have a presence on (cont.)

7

> **?**
>
> **Did you know?**
>
> The average Facebook user has 130 friends.
>
> More than 25 billion pieces of content (web links, news stories, blog posts, notes, photo albums, etc.) is shared each month.
>
> Over 300,000 users helped translate the site through the translations application.
>
> More than 150 million people engage with Facebook on external websites every month.
>
> Two-thirds of comScore's US Top 100 websites and half of comScore's Global Top 100 websites have integrated with Facebook.
>
> There are more than 100 million active users currently accessing Facebook through their mobile devices.
>
> People that access Facebook via mobile are twice as active than non-mobile users (think about that when designing your Facebook page).
>
> The average Facebook user is connected to 60 pages, groups and events.
>
> People spend over 500 billion minutes per month on Facebook.
>
> There are more than 1 million entrepreneurs and developers from 180 countries on Facebook.

Social media and social tagging sites your website should have a presence on (cont.)

- **Plaxo** (www.plaxo.com) Join Plaxo to organise your contacts and stay updated, with feeds from Digg, Amazon.com, Delicious and more.

- **Bebo** (www.bebo.com) Bebo is the largest UK social network, bringing together much of the same mixed demographics group that you tend to find on Facebook.

- **LinkedIn** (www.linkedin.com) LinkedIn is a popular networking site where alumni, business associates, recent graduates and other professionals connect online.

?

Did you know?

There are more than 70 million LinkedIn users worldwide.

Members of LinkedIn come from more than 200 countries from every continent.

LinkedIn is available in six native languages – English, French, German, Italian, Portuguese and Spanish.

80% of companies use LinkedIn as a recruitment tool.

A new member joins LinkedIn every second.

LinkedIn receives almost 12 million unique visitors per day.

- **It increases your network** The wider your circle of customers and individuals, the more chances there are that you could add to your business. Twitter, for example, gets more than 300,000 new users every day. Social networking can help you to increase the circle of people you can influence to buy your products. Each person you contact is almost sure to know a few others who would also be interested in your product or service. While social networking, you can always ask for their help to give you a few pointers and e-mail addresses and then you will be on your way to contacting many more individuals who could benefit your business.

- **It builds togetherness** When you are into social networking, you are able to build a personal relationship with people and, because of the one-to-one nature of it, you can get to know their needs and requirements better. You can help them out with their queries and doubts and thus build a relationship of trust where the person considers you an expert in such matters. They will, in turn, take this awareness with them and communicate it to their friends and social circle who, in turn, may contact you for your professional inputs. Forums are a good way to meet more people, as you will always find people in forums who have problems that you may just be able to solve.

- **It improves your online reputation** Once it has been established that there are certain areas where you have an in-depth knowledge which can be of use to many people, you will have made a reputation for yourself online. This will probably lead to people recognising you and your business as a reliable brand. You will have done this without any advertising and also gained a reputation for knowledge and reliability.

- **It is a low-cost form of marketing** Once you have been in contact with a number of interested people, you can use this to your advantage and give them information about your products and services either by e-mail or by directing them to your website, which has all the details of your business and what it offers. The cost of marketing in this way is low, almost zero, and limited to the cost of your keeping your websites constantly updated.

◀ **The benefits of social networking**

? 7

Did you know?

Twitter's web platform only accounts for a quarter of its users – 75% use third-party apps.

There are currently 110 million users of Twitter's services.

Twitter receives 180 million unique visits each month.

There are more than 600 million searches on Twitter every day.

Twitter started as a simple SMS-text service.

Over 60% of Twitter use is outside the US.

There are more than 50,000 third-party apps for Twitter.

Twitter has donated access to all of its tweets to the Library of Congress for research and preservation.

More than a third of users access Twitter via their mobile phone.

SEO and directories

▶

Your page rank (PR) is determined, largely, by the number of backlinks that lead to your site from other sites. Although your page rank is not what it used to be because it has been abused so much, it still carries a certain amount of weight with Google and is taken fully into account by Yahoo! and Bing.

The reason your page rank is so important is that each link you get from another site counts as a vote of confidence for your site – a little like being endorsed by your friends for how well you did something. The more links you have, the greater the endorsement. Also, the more trusted the site that links to you, the more value that link has (just like a real-life endorsement from someone important).

One-way links (that is, sites linking to you without you linking back to them) are valued because they link to you without the expectation of anything in return, so these links count more.

All this oversimplifies a complex issue but serves our purposes well enough. Just as in real life an endorsement from someone important who expects nothing back from you in return counts more than a tit-for-tat recommendation, on the Web, quality sites that link to you are considered more important to your site than links you exchange or links you buy.

As a matter of fact, buying links in an attempt to artificially bolster your site's page rank is likely to end up in you being penalised by Google, which is counterproductive.

So, if you are looking to find quality, one-way links, where do you begin? Spending hours researching likely websites and contacting individual webmasters with a request to post a link to your site is likely to amount to a huge waste of your time for the number of links it will actually give you. A lot of webmasters are under the same pressure of time (and the need to obtain a good page rank) that you are, so why should they bother?

This leaves the only other viable option and the subject of this section – directories.

There are thousands of directories on the Web that need content in order to be viable. They work hard to attract visitors and could give you both links and traffic in return. There is no shortcut to adding your website to the directories. If you hire an agency to do the work for you, you should expect to pay a minimum of £300 and, depending on which one you hire, you will never be 100 per cent sure of the work it's done.

If you decide to do it yourself, you will save money and at least know it's been done right, but it does involve an investment of your time. If you decide to do it this way, here's how you should approach it.

- **Timetable it** Allow a certain number of minutes each day for directory link building.

- **Standardise it** Have your description, URL and relevant information in a Word file that you can simply paste and copy from. You will be amazed at how much time this actually saves you!

- **Make a progress list** Write down which directories you have submitted to and when. Directories are always edited by humans. Some will take just a few weeks to list your site, others six months. You need to be thorough, methodical and meticulous and, above all, patient. This is a long-term link-building strategy that will pay off. If your site is listed on 1000 directories, for instance, you will achieve at least an extra 1000 unique visitors each month from them.

- **Work from a directory page rank position** Those with the highest page ranks should be top of your list and those with the lowest at the bottom.

The majority of directories are free, but you may have to pay for some. I suggest that you leave those until the very end. It is enough that you are spending time and effort creating listings right now without having to pay as well.

? 7

Did you know?

When you are searching for directories, it may get hard to find anything good past the top few results. You still have thousands of small directories to find, though, and there are many advanced search features to help you find diamonds in the rough.

SEO and directories (cont.)

Boosting your online marketing

1 Create a profile on each of the social networking websites mentioned in this chapter. Make sure that you fill out your profile completely on each one, providing a link back to your website.

2 Make a detailed list of all of the directories you will need your website to be included in.

3 Create a realistic, daily timetable to actually place your website in each of those directories.

It is important to realise that your business or website will fall into many categories. That being said, I will use an SEO-orientated website as an example. The website is about webmaster resources, search engines, business to business, marketing, small business … Also, don't forget location-specific directories.

Small business example

I can find directories about any of the terms above and justify my being included in them. One of the top ways to find these directories is to perform a search for the type of directory or market you are looking to list well in. For example, I will use the 'small business' idea to find small business directories.

If you perform a search for a small business directory or directories and fall short there still are many similar options. A small touch of creativity will allow you to find these 'hidden' directories. Search for phrases such as:

small business + resources

small business + add url

small business + submit

small business + submit url

small business + websites

small business + directory

small business + list

Finding directories in the open directory project

Using the above techniques or similar ones, you should be able to find many Web directories and many incoming links. Another way to find directories, though, is to search for them specifically within the open directory project (**www.dmoz.org**).

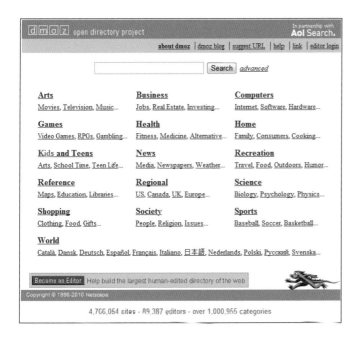

A Google search such as 'site:dmoz.org inurl:directories' would return directories.

In addition to searching for general directories, you can search for more *specific* directories, such as art directories. The search 'site:dmoz.org inurl:directories art' would include all pages with directories in the URL and 'art' in the page copy.

The Yahoo! Directory (at: **http://dir.yahoo.com/**) may also be a good place to look to find other directories.

Advanced SEO

Introduction

Everything we have looked at so far has required no knowledge of anything beyond your ability to read and write English. Not all SEO techniques are as straightforward to implement. Advanced SEO techniques, as the name suggests, require a little more hands-on tinkering. Luckily, there is nothing truly complicated in this and the step-by-step instructions will help you to achieve even the most seemingly complicated of SEO tasks.

For your information

What is advanced SEO? As the name suggests 'advanced SEO' is the kind of search engine optimisation work that you start to do on your website once you have carried out all the other SEO work we have looked at up to now. The work itself is not overtly technical, but does require a little knowledge of basic website programming and how code works.

What you'll do

Find out if you need to employ advanced SEO techniques

Learn how to kick-start your site's presence with a robots text (robots.txt) file

Find out how to avoid a duplicate contents penalty for your website

Find out if your content has been scraped (i.e. stolen)

Set things straight if your content has been scraped

Find out how page rank (PR) is calculated

Balance your SEO with a well thought out PPC

Optimise your website to work with other languages

Learn the value of intelligence about your competitor's websites

Find out about linking strategies that help your SEO

Score your linking actions

Do you need to employ advanced SEO techniques?

See also

See 'How to find out if your website has been indexed' in Chapter 5.

Although relatively straightforward, advanced SEO techniques always take more time to employ and are more fiddly when it comes to dealing with each section than the ones covered so far. That is why it is always good to assess if you really need to get into them.

To do this, check the following.

- Your website's visitor numbers, month-on-month, via your Google Analytics account. If your website shows a steady increase in visitor numbers each month, then the chances are that everything in terms of your SEO is working fine and tinkering with advanced SEO techniques will give you only a marginal increase. That does not mean you should not go ahead and do some of the things we cover in this chapter, but, if time is an issue (and it usually is), then it is better to prioritise and leave these techniques to be revisited at a later date.

- Check to see if the number of pages for your website fluctuates wildly in the indexes of the three main search engines by going to each one and inputting **site:http://www.mysitename.com** in the search box. If the number of pages shown fluctuates from day to day or month to month, you need to get to grips with some advanced SEO techniques.

If you have never heard of it before, a robots text file (commonly referred to as robots.txt file) is a couple of short lines of code designed to help indexing robots know how to treat your site.

The first logical question is, 'Why?' First, let's get rid of the myths. A robots.txt file will *not* help your site to rise in the search engine results pages (the position your site appears in lists of results for certain search terms). Nor will it make a search engine bot index more pages than it normally would. As a matter of fact, a search engine bot *not* finding a robots. txt file on your site will just assume that it can go anywhere it likes and it will index every page.

So, why go to the bother of creating one? There are three good reasons to do so.

- A robots.txt file tells search engine bots where *not* to go on your site, therefore keeping some directories or files out of the search engines' databases.

- Not having a robots.txt file can mean unnecessary 404s ('page not found' error) reports are returned as the search engine bots try to crawl password-protected directories. This masks the real 404s and affects the way that your site performs in terms of organic SEO standing.

- The presence of a robots.txt file signals a site that is well constructed and meticulous in the way it communicates with search engine bots. By pressing 'the right buttons' with them, you also make sure that they will perform optimally on your website.

The second logical question is, 'How do I create one?'

First, go to **Start>All programs>Accessories>Notepad** on your computer. In the blank Notepad file, type the following:

```
User-agent: *
Allow:
```

How to kick-start your site's presence with a robots text (robots.txt) file

8

How to kick-start your site's presence with a robots text (robots.txt) file (cont.)

If you have a sitemap uploaded to the root directory of your website, then list it here by adding:

Sitemap: http://www.yourwebsitename.com/sitemap.xml

Finally, and for good measure, include:

User-Agent: msnbot
Crawl-Delay: 20

This asks the MSN bot to slow down in its indexing, as it can sometimes try to index website pages too fast and cause server timeouts.

If you have done all of the above (and provided you are not protecting any directories) your robots.txt file should look like this:

User-agent: *
Allow:
Sitemap: http://www.yourwebsitename.com/sitemap.xml

User-Agent: msnbot
Crawl-Delay: 20

Now save the file as a text file (with a .txt extension) with the name 'robots.txt' (please note, it's 'robots' not 'robot') and use your FTP client to send it to the root directory of your site.

If, for any reason, you want to exclude particular pages from being indexed (or even entire directories from being indexed), then add the following command:

User-agent: *
Disallow: /mydirectoryname/myfilename/ # This is my description of this
Disallow: /myfilename/ # these will soon disappear
Disallow: /myname.html

```
User-Agent: *
Disallow: /music?
Disallow: /widgets/radio?
Disallow: /show_ads.php

Disallow: /affiliate/
Disallow: /affiliate_redirect.php
Disallow: /affiliate_sendto.php
Disallow: /campaignlink.php
Disallow: /delivery.php

Disallow: /music/*noredirect/

Disallow: /harming/humans
Disallow: /harm/to/self

Allow: /
```

How to kick-start your site's presence with a robots text (robots.txt) file (cont.)

The above command stops all search engine bots from indexing the directory you specify and any file starting with the name you specify in the first 'Disallow' command line. The disallow command lines after that need to be included only if there is a specific file you do not want to be indexed and you need to give the specific file name and a specific site page you do not want indexed and, again, you need to give the page file name. If these do not apply, you only need to include:

User-agent: *
Disallow: /mydirectoryname/myfilename/ # This is my description of this

It is good practice to get into the habit of describing what disallowed pages are because, even if you are the only person dealing with your site, two months and a few hundreds of files later, you may well forget.

Decide if there are any areas of your website you need to protect from indexing and, in Notepad, copy and paste the code given above, replace 'mydirectory/name/myfilename' with the directory and file name you want to protect and then save it as a .txt file. Upload it to the root directory of your website via FTP.

Did you know?

Once you have created your robots.txt file you need to check it's valid. Although a robots.txt file is not complicated it is sometimes easy to make a mistake in the syntax invalidating its effectiveness.

Here's what you do to check: After you have created your robots.txt file and uploaded it to your domain go to **http://www. sxw.org.uk/computing/robots/ check.html** and type in your website address in the field box there. Click on the submit button to check.

8

How to avoid a duplicate contents penalty for your website

It's no secret that duplicate content can hurt your website's standing with search engines. The questions in relation to this are, 'How does duplicate content from within your own website come about?' and 'What effect will it have and what can I do about it?'

If your website is dynamic and has tracking IDs and session IDs, then it means that user information goes through them, which can result in the unnecessary duplication of your site's content in the main Google index.

The Google bot indexes each page it finds and dynamically generated session IDs or tracking IDs can generate a number of similar pages, which will be indexed. At the same time, bear in mind that the dynamic parameters of session and tracking IDs result in URLs that have a string of characters, making it difficult to index them properly (which is why they call them search engine-unfriendly URLs). This is a problem that you will have to cope with as a webmaster.

Thankfully, there are concrete solutions to both issues.

First, regarding the duplicate content problem, determine where your duplicate problem originates from and consider using permanent (301) redirects through the .htaccess file in your site's root folder. If your site is a dynamic website, it will be hosted, usually, on an Apache server. Apache servers have a file in the root directory of each website they host labelled .htaccess and this file contains commands that usually tell the server and search engines how to treat a website.

To change this file you will need to use FTP and access the root directory of your website. Locate the .htaccess file and download it to your desktop. Once you have it, you can open it using either Notepad or an HTML editor program, such Dreamweaver. When it is open, write the following command line in there, making sure that you substitute the actual domain name of your website for 'mywebsitename':

Timesaver tip

It's a good idea to let search engines find and index your content first before distributing it out on an RSS feed. This sends a signal to search engines that you are the original source before they find it on other sites. To speed up this process you can use a tool like Ping-O-Matic (**http://www.pingomatic.com**) to update search engines and feed sites that your content has been updated and it's ready.

```
RewriteEngine On
RewriteCond %{HTTP_HOST} ^www.mywebsitename\.com
[nc]
RewriteRule (.*) mywebsitename\.com/$1 [R=301,L]
```

The command tells search engines that the two versions
of your website – the **www.mywebsite.com** one and the **http://
mywebsite.com** one – are exactly the same and should be
treated as one. That will take care of expected duplicate
content. If you are not sure where duplicate content arises
from, however, it may be worth your while to create a Google
Webmaster account (at: **www.google.com/webmasters**) if you
haven't already.

Once you have a Google Webmaster Tools account, log into it
and make sure that Google references your site as either **www.
mydomain.com** *or* **http://mydomain.com**. Which one you decide
to go for will depend on the number of back links there are to
one or the other and the number of pages indexed by Google
(Google treats www and http:// domain addresses as separate,
despite them being the same domain, though recent upgrades
are beginning to take canonicalisation into account).

This should take care of the issue of duplicate content.

Now for the indexing problem. There are various patches or
modules that can be applied to a dynamic website and help to
turn dynamic URLs into search engine-friendly ones. If you have
a website that is run by a content management system such as
Joomla or WordPress, it can become very easy to apply a patch
to make sure that the strings of numbers the website generates
for each one of its pages turn into readable words.

By taking action on these two points, you will help ensure that
your site is indexed properly and avoid being penalised for
duplicate content.

How to avoid a duplicate contents penalty for your website (cont.)

?

Did you know?

32% of websites suffer
from plagiarised content.

28% of large websites
reiterate much of their
content through re-writes.

The Google Panda search
algorithm update has
been designed specifically
to target websites with
plagiarised or repetitive
content and drop their
rankings. To date this has
affected some 200,000
websites. This makes the
content you have on your
website one of the central
elements of your SEO and
SEM strategy.

8

Has your Web content been scraped (i.e. stolen?)

As we have been talking about duplicate content and advanced SEO techniques, it is worth discussing a problem that arises on the Web and has to do with stolen content. With over 200,000 websites joining the Web each day, it is safe to assume that not all are going to be value-loaded, high-quality, visitor-enriching websites, which means some are going to be what Google classes as spam sites.

1. To see if there is duplicate content of your Web pages out there, go to Copyscape (**copyscape.com**), enter the URL of each page the content of which you are checking and see what the results are.

2. Hopefully, beyond your own site no other pages will show up. The nightmare begins the moment you find sites you do not recognise that are using your content. Should this happen, follow the steps in the next section to find out what you need to do to make sure that this does not happen to you and, if it does, what you can do to set matters straight.

A spam site uses bogus or stolen keyword-rich content to drive traffic to its pages and make money from PPC ads, banner impressions, paid advertising and even link selling. That means many of the best-performing sites for a given search engine query may become the target of stolen content (also called site scraping), which is then used to drive traffic to the bogus site. That means your legit site may often lose precious places on the organic search engine results page, be penalised for duplicate content and even, in some extreme cases, be banned.

Content is stolen using an automated technique known as scraping. Essentially, scraping employs a Web-based program that visits websites just like a search engine bot and steals their content in seconds.

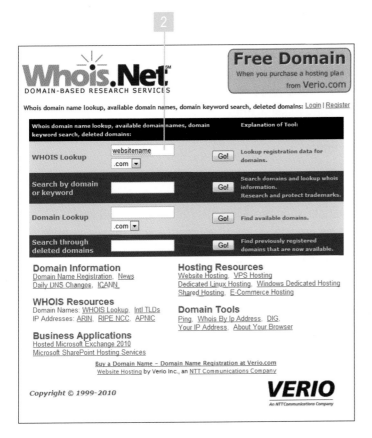

Prepare a letter of notification to send to the hosting company. A Digital Millennium Copyright Act (DMCA) Take Down letter has been included here to give you an idea of what you should say and how you should say it.

My name is [Insert name] and I am the [Insert title] of [Insert company name]. A website that your company hosts (according to Whois information) is infringing on at least one copyright owned by my company.

An article was copied on to your servers without permission. The original [Article/photo], to which we own the exclusive copyrights, can be found at:

[Provide website URL]

The unauthorised and infringing copy can be found at:

[Provide website URL]

1 Visit the infringing sites, get their contact details and send them an e-mail explaining that you are the legitimate owner of the content they are using on their websites. Either politely ask them to remove the content they are infringing on (make sure you point out the exact pages concerned by providing the URLs for them) or, alternatively, explain that you are willing to licence the use of that content for a fee (decide what is acceptable to you and how you would like to be paid). Make sure you give the webmasters reasonable deadlines to comply by (make it more than 72 hours, just to be on the safe side) and a means of contacting you.

2 Next, prepare your fallback plan. Visit Whois (**www.whois. net**), input the URL of the website that you have found is using your content and find out who the site belongs to exactly and, most importantly, where it is hosted. The hosting server will be detailed at the bottom of the WHOIS report on the website.

8

Setting things straight if your content has been scraped (cont.)

3 Wait until the deadline you have given to the infringing website's webmaster has expired. It may well be that they contact you before that happens, but, if no one does, do not contact the company again.

4 Your next step is to send your prepared letter of notification (shown opposite) to the hosting company, identifying the owner of the website, the infringing pages and content and letting the company know that you have already contacted the webmaster of the infringing site. Ask the hosting company to either take down the content (if it is a page or two) or take down the website (if the entire site contains content that belongs to you).

5 What will happen next is that, within just a few hours of receiving your notification, the hosting company will comply by taking down the offending pages or suspending the account of the offending website.

This letter is official notification under Section 512(c) of the Digital Millennium Copyright Act ('DMCA') and I seek the removal of the aforementioned infringing material from your servers. I request that you immediately notify the infringer of this notice and inform them of their duty to remove the infringing material immediately, and notify them to cease any further posting of infringing material to your server in the future.

Please also be advised that law requires you, as a service provider, to remove or disable access to the infringing materials upon receiving this notice. Under US law, a service provider, such as yourself, enjoys immunity from a copyright lawsuit provided that you act with deliberate speed to investigate and rectify ongoing copyright infringement. If service providers do not investigate and remove or disable the infringing material, this immunity is lost. Therefore, in order for you to remain immune from a copyright infringement action, you will need to investigate and ultimately remove or otherwise disable the infringing material from your servers with all due speed should the direct infringer, your client, not comply immediately.

I am providing this notice in good faith and with the reasonable belief that rights my company owns are being infringed. Under penalty of perjury I certify that the information contained in the notification is both true and accurate and I have the authority to act on behalf of the owner of the copyright(s) involved.

Should you wish to discuss this with me please contact me directly.

Thank you.

[Your name]

[Address]
[Phone]
[E-mail]

Infringement of intellectual property rights (IPR) is a serious crime and is illegal in Europe, Australia and the USA. If the hosting company is based in any of these countries, they will have, as part of their standard operating procedure, a process for reporting infringement of intellectual property rights on the websites they host. As a precaution and to save time, contact the host and find out what its procedure is for reporting intellectual property rights violations and what the requirements are for proof of ownership.

In cases of online infringement of intellectual property rights, Google has a reporting page where content can be removed by them (**http://www.google.com/support/bin/static.py?page=+s. cs8ts=1114905**).

Once the content has been removed, make sure that you check with Copyscape regularly – at least once a month – to ensure you do not fall victim to something like this again. Remember, the more successful your site is thanks to your SEO efforts, the more likely it is to have its content stolen.

If the website is down because its account has been suspended, you will find that the website owner(s) will be in touch quickly enough to negotiate with you so that the website can be reinstated.

How is page rank (PR) calculated?

When you calculate the page rank for a given page on your site, you must take into account all the links leading to it. This includes links that come from other pages *within* your site and links that come from *outside* your site. There is a mathematical formula for this is and it is:

$$PR(A) = (1-d) + d(PR(t1)/C(t1) + ... + PR(tn)/C(tn))$$

It is this equation that is used to calculate a page's ranking. It's the original one that was published when page ranking was being developed, so it is more than probable Google now uses a more advanced variation of it, but it isn't telling anyone what it is. It doesn't matter, though, as this equation is good enough for our purposes.

In the equation, 't1 – tn' are pages linking to page A, 'C' is the number of outbound links that a page has and 'd' is a damping factor, usually set to 0.85.

We can think of it in a simpler way:

- a page's page ranking = 0.15 + 0.85 (a 'share' of the page ranking of every page that links to it)
- 'share' = the linking page's page rank divided by the number of outbound links on that page.

A page 'votes' an amount of a page's ranking on to each page that it links to. The amount of this ranking that it has to vote with is a little less than its own value (its own value 0.85, which really means that it confers about 85 per cent of its value). This value is shared equally between all the pages that it links to, which means it does not get watered down by the number of pages it links to provided there is a certain consistency to the linking strategy.

Beyond a certain number of links on a page, Google begins to suspect that you are either selling links or running a link farm. Either way, the page rank you confer begins to drop in value. From this, we can conclude that a link from a page with PR4 and 5 outbound links is worth more in terms of how it 'votes' than a link from a page with PR8 and 100 outbound links, which are seen to vote indiscriminately. The page rank of a page that links to yours is important, but the number of links on that page is also important. The more links there are on a page, the less page rank value your page will receive from it, unless, thematically, there is such a close link that having a link there makes perfect sense.

The Google algorithm – PageRank – is tremendously complicated and designed to emulate human intelligence. If the value differences between PR1, PR2 ... PR10 were equal, then the conclusion that the number of links on a page waters down its vote would hold up, but, within the SEO world, many experts believe the values between PR1 and PR10 (the maximum) are set on a logarithmic scale. Nobody outside Google really knows how true this is, but the many tests we have carried out do seem to bear it out. What this means is that it takes a lot more additional share of the page rank for a page to move up to the next level than it did to move up from the previous level to its present one. So, if it took a few hundred hits a day and 1000 back links to bring your site's page ranking from 1 to 2, it takes significantly more work and time to bring it to 3 and so on. The result of this is that a link from a PR8 page with *lots* of outbound links is worth more than a link from a PR4 page that has only a *few* outbound links.

One urban myth regarding SEO is that, when a page votes its page rank value to other pages, it gives away part of its own page rank. While it is good practice to link to other pages, as if that were true – in which case, you are building links of true value – there is absolutely no truth whatsoever in the myth. A Web page's own page rank is not reduced by the value that it is voting to other pages.

The million-dollar question now is, how do you go about getting some idea of your page's true value?

How is page rank (PR) calculated? (cont.)

Did you know?

If you are using Firefox as a browser, a handy add-on to have is Google Toolbar. The Google Toolbar scans Google's database for websites and displays any websites you visit, real PageRank. To install the Google Toolbar go to **http://www.google.com/toolbar/** and click on the download link. The installation process lasts just a few minutes after which you may have to restart your browser.

8

How is page rank (PR) calculated? (cont.)

OK, here goes nothing:

- calculate page A's page ranking from the value of its inbound links

- calculate page B's page ranking from the value of its inbound links.

You need to repeat this process for every page that links to other pages, so, if you have, for instance, page A linking to pages B, C and D, you will have to do it for each one. In each case, you are creating a built-in uncertainty because the value of the other pages is only guessed at rather than calculated, so it is not entirely accurate.

The only way to arrive at an approximation that is close enough is to take the new values and start again. Each time you run the calculation, the uncertainty decreases incrementally and you are – if you run a sufficient number of calculations – going to reach the page's true value.

To give you an idea of Google's calculating power, this is done between 50 and 60 times for just 2 pages and they do it for *every* page that they index. The reiteration of the calculation stops the moment the new values produced stop being significantly different, which means when we are approaching a normalised value.

The calculation then goes through a further refining process. This part of Google's formula is secret. It creates variables that, when calculated, produce a page's true page ranking. Now, if you think that, armed with this knowledge, you will be able to go ahead and calculate the page ranking of each page on your site, be aware, what you are *really* calculating is the proportional value the Google algorithm takes into account when it starts to calculate a page's true ranking.

Link Popularity Check Tool

SeoCentro designed this search engine optimization tool for to check link popularity from websites. The Link Popularity analysis program will search Google, Yahoo, AllTheWeb, AltaVista, and MSN to determine how many pages are linking to your web page.
Bookmark this page!

How popular is your web site?

example: **www.host.com** or **host.com**

www.weddingrings.net — URL: 1

www.alisa-miller.com — URL: 2 *

— URL: 3 *

Send report to an e-mail address (optional).

— Email

☑ Send in HTML format.

8576
Please enter the **access code** as displayed above.

8756 — Access code

[Submit]

* The second and third URL are optional.

Related links

- Buy the Link Popularity script!
- Add the Link Popularity Tool to your web site FREE!

Try it yourself. Use **www.seocentro.com/tools/search-engines/ link-popularity.html** to calculate the one-way inbound links to your site and even to individual pages on your site. Follow the instructions above regarding how to calculate the page ranks.

URL	Total	Google	Yahoo!	Live	AllTheWeb	AltaVista
www.alisa-miller.com	198	4	90	16	0	88
www.poor.com	233	0	44	98	44	47
www.okay.com	478	5	16	426	15	16
www.fun.com	1515	0	389	705	200	221
www.popreport.com	3471	26	1560	427	716	742
www.lamaleta.org	5177	25	1490	52	1800	1810
www.weddingrings.net	6809	9	4400	200	0	2200
www.hostinglogia.com	11377	75	3630	22	3820	3830
www.widexl.com	13052	132	4070	5780	1470	1600
www.softhome.net	13345	75	5410	1150	3270	3440
www.golber.com	20111	46	16100	365	1790	1810
www.seocentro.com	20140	87	7670	383	5980	6020
www.popular.com	26970	327	482	25700	229	232
www.horror.com	28197	727	8340	14900	1410	2820
www.electroniccottage.com	28563	213	9160	4280	7450	7460
www.artquest.com	32508	208	12600	3860	7870	7970
www.update.com	32618	188	3610	25400	1710	1710
www.micex.com	35650	1560	15200	8500	5190	5200
www.bnn.nl	60600	400	23500	13800	11000	11900
www.jobpilot.de	117961	461	56000	24800	18300	18400
www.manchesteronline.co.uk	167140	1040	69400	16900	39800	40000
www.bmw.com	441850	1450	219000	83500	68600	69300
www.realestateabc.com	531820	2520	253000	18300	129000	129000
www.hosting.com	578650	2800	14700	549000	5550	6600
www.hotscripts.com	1831570	6570	908000	264000	325000	328000
www.apache.org	10521000	21000	5740000	1630000	1440000	1460000
www.microsoft.com	392283200	73200	5460000	292000000	3290000	2330000
www.mysql.com	99130000	1020000	75500000	1610000	10400000	10600000
www.yahoo.com	200910000	1980000	118000000	1930000	35100000	39800000
www.google.com	469650000	2730000	272000000	42300000	75300000	2730000

0 to 250 references
251 to 1000 references
1001 to 2,500 references
2,501 to 10,000 references
10,001 to 50,000 references
50,001 to 1,000,000 references
1,000,001 to 10,000,000 references
10,000,000 references and up

back

Balancing your SEO with a well thought out PPC

See also

See Chapter 4.

The main point of SEO is that you do not have to rely on paid advertising, such as Google AdWords, which is called pay-per-click (PPC), in order to drive traffic to your website. However, a pay-per-click campaign can come in handy when:

- you want to cover a gap in your SEO fast

- you want your website to appear for some very specific keywords and these are time-sensitive, which means that you cannot afford to wait for your SEO efforts to kick in

- something has changed and your main keyword has stopped delivering traffic to you (usually because your main competitors have stepped up their campaigns and are now ahead of you on the search engine results pages).

It is worth bearing a few things in mind:

- any organic SEO effort, to achieve its goal, requires a certain amount of time

- even the best optimised of sites can be temporarily knocked off their perches

- a PPC contingency fund should always be in place for just such scenarios, when your website just *has* to be in the public eye on the first page of Google for a very specific reason and a very specific keyword.

Organic SEO work should always be your first policy. It lends your site credibility if it comes up on the organic search engine page results, it leads to a lot of targeted traffic for very little cost and impacts positively on the way your website is perceived.

Do not run your website blindfolded. Make it part of your daily routine to be aware of events that may affect traffic to your organic search engine page results and be prepared to take action when necessary via your PPC spend. Routinely go to Google.co.uk and test to see how your website performs for specific keywords.

The Web tends to be so Anglocentric it is easy to forget that a large portion of it is *not* based on English-speakers and it may prove very accessible to your business message. Although your website may be hosted in the UK and targeting a predominantly home-based potential audience, there could still also be opportunities further afield. This will be useful to you if you:

- are trading in goods or services that can easily travel outside the UK

- have content on your website that is of use to people living in other countries

- need to start promoting your website to markets outside your core one.

Whether you are selling goods or services, you are online precisely because you want to attract a global audience in a cost-effective way and the Web is perfect for that. All this means that, in your SEO efforts, you cannot afford to ignore search engines in other languages. The trick here is not to try and sell your Web products and services in other languages to the locals of the countries in question, but, rather, get those locals to your website where they can do business with you in English.

The question, of course, is how do you go about it? Well, for a start, you do not need to launch new micro-sites or translate your entire site and its contents into another language in order to submit it to specific foreign language search engines. You do need, however, to translate your website's homepage. This could then be given a URL something like **www.mysitename.com/fr**, for French, a similar page for German and so on.

Your first step is to decide which countries you will need to target. That decision will be guided by analysing the traffic from your Google Analytics account, which will show you if other countries' nationals are finding your site. If, for instance, you discover that 10 per cent of your traffic is coming from France, you could translate your site's home page into French and submit it to the French language database of each of the major search engines – Google, Yahoo! and MSN.

Optimise your website to work with other languages

8

Optimise your website to work with other languages (cont.)

1. In the case of Google, visit its website (at: **www.google. com/addurl/?continue=/addurl** and submit the URL of the language you are promoting on your website.

2. If you are not proficient in the target language, you may need to hire a translator or use Google's online translation service: (at **www. google.com/language_tools**), though do bear in mind that this is still in beta mode and, when it comes to idiomatic expressions in English, can give some imprecise results.

Google — Add your URL to Google

Home
About Google
Advertising Programs
Business Solutions
Webmaster Info
▸ Submit Your Site

Find on this site
Search

Share your place on the net with us.

We add and update new sites to our index each time we crawl the web, and we invite you to submit your URL here. We do not add all submitted URLs to our index, and we cannot make any predictions or guarantees about when or if they will appear.

Please enter your full URL, including the `http://` prefix. For example: `http://www.google.com/`. You may also add comments or keywords that describe the content of your page. These are used only for our information and do not affect how your page is indexed or used by Google.

Please note. Only the top-level page from a host is necessary; you do not need to submit each individual page. Our crawler, Googlebot, will be able to find the rest. Google updates its index on a regular basis, so updated or outdated link submissions are not necessary. Dead links will fade out of our index on our next crawl when we update our entire index.

URL:
Comments:
Optional: To help us distinguish between sites submitted by individuals and those automatically entered by software robots, please type the squiggly letters shown here in the box below.

pImpi

Add URL

Need to remove a site from Google? For more information, click here.

©2006 Google · Home · About Google · We're Hiring · Site Map

1
2

Translated search

Type a search phrase in your language. Google will find results in other languages and translate them for you to read.

Search for: [   ] Translate and Search

Search pages written in:
◉ Automatically selected languages
○ Specific languages

My language:
English ▾

Example 1. Search for Bern tourist information.
2. We translate your query into French and German, and find French and German results.
3. Finally, we translate the French and German results back into your language.

Translate text

Spanish ▾ » English ▾ Translate

Translate a web page

http://www.mywebsitename.com
English ▾ » Spanish ▾ Translate

Use the Google Interface in Your Language

Set the Google homepage, messages, and buttons to display in your selected language via our Preferences page. Google currently offers the following interface languages:

• Afrikaans	• Estonian	• Kazakh	• Occitan	• Sundanese
• Akan	• Faroese	• Kinyarwanda	• Oriya	• Swahili
• Albanian	• Filipino	• Kirundi	• Oromo	• Swedish
• Amharic	• Finnish	• Klingon	• Pashto	• Tajik
• Arabic	• French	• Korean	• Persian	• Tamil
• Armenian	• Frisian	• Kurdish	• Pirate	• Tatar
• Azerbaijani	• Galician	• Kyrgyz	• Polish	• Telugu
• Basque	• Georgian	• Laothian	• Portuguese (Brazil)	• Thai
• Belarusian	• German	• Latin	• Portuguese (Portugal)	• Tigrinya
• Bengali	• Greek	• Latvian	• Punjabi	• Tonga
• Bihari	• Guarani	• Lingala	• Quechua	• Turkish

Working on the details of your website's SEO, it is all too easy to forget that all your efforts, skill and the knowledge you gather here are only as good as your competitors' SEO efforts, skills and websites permit.

This should not be as shocking as it sounds. Yes, you know exactly what you need to do in order to optimise your website for fast indexing, in-depth indexing and a high position in the search engines' results pages, but (and it is a really big but), if your competitors' websites are older than yours, have a higher page ranking than your site and have already built up traffic for the relevant search terms, knocking them out of that position is going to be a pretty tall order. Luckily it is not impossible. Here is what you need to do.

Understand what your competitors are doing

First of all, you need to realise that, in order for your site to appear higher than your competitors' sites for similar search terms you don't just need to emulate them but clearly understand what they are doing, then do it better. Here we will see how we can analyse each aspect in order to reach the correct conclusion. I want to also stress that each analysis run has a built-in error factor and imprecision, so it will not be as conclusive as we would like (I will give an example in a moment), so it is important to tackle them all in order to build up as comprehensive a picture as possible. In terms of the imprecisions we will encounter, here is an example.

The value of intelligence about your competitors' websites

Timesaver tip

Gathering intelligence on your competitors should be part of your strategy. This takes time and cannot be applied to every single website. Some websites will be below yours in terms of SEO performance. It is useful to have a means of sorting out the ones you will be competing against from the ones you outperform without having to go through the time-consuming online intelligence gathering steps. To get an overview of the data you need go to **http://websitegrader.com/** and input in the field the URL of the website you want to check. You can also input your own, but it's not necessary. What you will get is a snapshot showing if that website is performing better than yours. If it is, it needs deeper analysis. If it isn't, you can ignore it.

The value of intelligence about your competitors' websites (cont.)

Timesaver tip

When you market your website you often need to do research on sites you visit, either because they are competition, or because you are thinking of partnering up. Here's a tip (you will need to have Firefox as your browser): go to http://www.quirk.biz/searchstatus/ and download 'Search Status'. Once installed it will appear at the bottom of your browsing bar. Click on it, and for every site you visit, SearchStatus lets you view its Google PageRank, Google Category, Alexa popularity ranking, Compete.com ranking, SEOmoz Linkscape mozRank, Alexa related links and backwards links from Google, Yahoo! And MSN. This means you can view not only the link importance of a site, but also its traffic importance.

Brilliant!

We will use the Internet Archive (at: www.archive.org) to check the true age of a website by seeing when it was first spidered. The thing is that it is only an indicator. If the site has been redesigned, then Google will have indexed it anew and so be out of sync, in terms of how old it thinks the site in its database is compared with the age the Internet Archive will report. I mention this here because it is important to understand not just the power of the tools we use for analysis but also their limitations.

Make a list of your main competitors

You may already have some idea as to who they are. If not, use the top three-four keywords in your industry and see which ten sites consistently rank on Google's first page for them. Draw up a list and that will be your target for analysis. You will need to have a column for each of the ten sites and include your own as it will help you to see how you really measure up.

Check a site's age

Let's begin by going to www.archive.org/index.php and, in the search box there, type the name of each of your competitors in turn. Make a note of when they were first indexed. The number of pages that have been indexed is also important as it indicates the importance of the website in terms of the traffic it attracts. There is little you can do to improve your website's age, so focus on your SEO activity and search engine marketing and wait.

Check a website's back links

One-way links and how these are indexed by search engines are an important indicator of a website's page ranking in that search engines' index. Each search engine has a different way in which it indexes back links and a different way of querying them. Here's how to query each search engine's index and see how many one-way back links each of your competitors has. Again, check your site either first or last at the following addresses to give you an idea.

- **Google: link:http://www.domainname.com**
- **Yahoo!: linkdomain:domainname.com**

- **Bing** copies Google in much of its approach. It has blocked queries from its search engine index, but will allow you to check the back links you have by going to its webmaster tools (at: **www.bing.com/toolbox/webmasters**). You will need to register an account there and input your website in order to be able to see the back links to your website, which are held in the Bing index.

Check the number of pages each site has indexed

The number of pages indexed by each search engine plays a vital role in the search results that each search engine will return on search queries relating to your site's content. If a search engine, for instance, has indexed just a handful of hundreds of pages on your site, then it will not be able to fully serve your content for relevant search terms. Use the following details to check each of the major search engines:

- **Google:** site:http://www.domainname.com

- **Yahoo!:** site:www.domainname.com

- **BING:** site:www.domainname.com

The value of intelligence about your competitors' websites (cont.)

Did you know?

If your website has not yet been indexed deeply by any (or all) of the major search engines you should:

- prepare a sitemap and upload it to your website
- create a few deep links leading from the homepage to other pages
- use a service such as Digg.com (at: **http://digg.com**) to publicise some on the content on your website.

The value of intelligence about your competitors' websites (cont.)

Check your page rank

Your page ranking is something that you can do little about. It is a combination of the site's age, how frequently it is updated, what traffic it gets and how many links, as well as the quality they each have. It is still necessary to know what it is, however. Here's how you check. Go to **www. digpagerank.com** and input **www.domainname.com**, then check each of the 45 data centres that come up there.

Another way to do this is to employ a Google Toolbar (at: **www.google.com/toolbar/ff/index.html**). It is free, allows you to check every website you visit and having it while visiting your own website can have a beneficial impact on its standing with Google (though only a small one, it must be said), as Google uses the Toolbar information it receives to check which sites are being visited, when and update trends on its database.

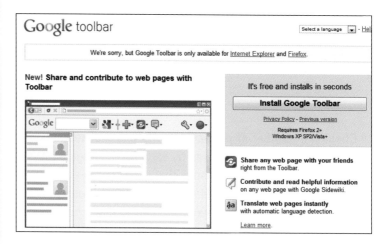

When you check on your competitors, it is always good to see what keywords or phrases they are targeting on their websites. Have a peak at their meta tags by visiting their websites and viewing the Web page sources.

How to check a website's meta tags

1. Go to the website you want to check.

2. Right click anywhere on the page.

3. From the drop down box select **View Page Source**.

4. Look at the lines of code which generate the web page. At the top part of the lines of code you will see the Meta Tags which now stand revealed.

5. Pay attention to Title, Description and Keywords. You can see what this page is using and you could even copy them for your site if it is similar.

The value of intelligence about your competitors' websites (cont.)

Linking strategies are a nightmare. On top of working hard to make sure your website is found by search engines, you now have to worry about a consistent linking strategy that will benefit your site's SEO standing.

The reason for doing this is that a site with no inbound or outbound links is deemed to be static and so of little real value and is then not ranked highly on the organic search engine results pages (SERPs).

OK, I know you will argue that this is not necessarily the case and you are 100 per cent right, but search engine robots cannot intelligently assess a site's real value. They can only go through the assessment of specific parameters and a website's link activity is one of them. So, unless search engine bots suddenly become intelligent, we are stuck with this.

For your information

If a web site links to your competitors it may also link to yours, and in order to find these potential link partners you can use search engines. Not so long ago Google was useful for getting a lot of back link information about a site. Recently Google's back link data is a lot less forthcoming and it now tends to show only a tiny percentage of the sites that are linking combined with a lot of internal link data. Whether the few websites Google shows us are the ones it finds important or whether they are in fact red herrings we cannot say for certain. I would assume the latter.

Currently Yahoo! is a better portal to check for back links. To generate a list of linking web sites on Yahoo! simply go to **http://www.yahoo.com** and type the following into the Yahoo search bar: **linkdomain:www. mycompetitorwebsite.com** (replace 'mycompetitorwebsite' with the domain name of the competitor website you are checking). This will deliver up to date link information as read by Yahoo!. The only downside with the information is that one site may appear many times if it is giving multiple links.

The good news is that there *are* things you can do to make sure your website ranks high up in the search engine results page. Let's look at each one in turn.

- **Create inbound links with specific anchor text** The fact is that you need to create links with a specific keyword text around them, either in the general description or the linking text. What happens is that your website becomes associated with the link words. For something that is really highly contested, such as the search term 'SEO', you merely get a boost in organic search engine results page rankings for using them. For low contention ratio words, such as those associated with a specific commercial website, you can, however, have your website associated with them so that when those looking for a specific product or service type the words into Google, your website automatically comes up high on the search engine results page.

- **Check the origins of inbound links** Essentially, apart from the fact that you need to make sure you get one-way links with the right description or anchor text, you also need to make sure that the page linking to you has a sufficiently high page rank (PR) itself. This then becomes a link of greater importance than, say, if the website linking to you is at PR0 level.

- **Have links from sites similar to yours** You'd be right in thinking that websites similar to yours are competing with yours. That is exactly why a link from a website similar to yours counts high with Google. The search engine takes the view, if a website that is your competitor still links to you, then your site is well worth the effort of linking to and, therefore, authoritative.

- **Have links from authoritative sites** In the search engine world, authoritative sites are like people. The word of professionals and academics is worth more than that of ordinary people. Similarly, a vote – which means a link from a .edu or a .gov site – counts more than a link from an ordinary site. If you can get one, or more, it is really worth the effort in terms of the effect it will have on the credibility and organic page ranking of your website.

Linking strategies that help your SEO

Jargon buster

Anchor text – The html text displayed and used in the link to your site eg: 'Click Here' – normally a blue underlined link.

8

Linking strategies that help your SEO (cont.)

Timesaver tip

Broken links on a website will adversely affect your SEO in the eyes of every search engine. Finding broken links and fixing them is a time consuming task.

This is where software comes to the rescue. Point your browser at **http://home. snafu.de/tilman/xenulink.** html and download and install the software. Use it to check your website for broken links and fix them: it really is that simple sometimes!

Increase the number of back links The number of one-way links leading back to your site is important. Broadly speaking, the more you have, the better, *but* remember all the points discussed above. That is, the keywords in the text link, description and reputation of the site linking to you are also important.

Anchor text with internal links Creating internal links should be part of your long-term cross-linking strategy. The anchor text for each of these links is also important.

Place text around an anchor link You already know that the text you have in a link is important. Google also places a lot of importance on the text that comes before and after a link. This is because it uses it to determine the relevancy of the link (and avoid link spamming) and the weight it will give it.

Watch the age of each link The age of a link is an important indication of its importance and relevancy. Older links are worth more and the older a link gets, the greater its weight. Many new links acquired suddenly suggests that you are buying links and so Google tends to look on them with suspicion.

Link with directories Certainly your site should be listed on dmoz (at: **www.dmoz.org**) and as many other directories as possible. Their PR, however, plays a critical role. If you have many links from directories at PR0 level, there is the possibility that you are buying links and therefore trying to manipulate your page rank score and SEO status, which is frowned on.

Increase the number of outgoing links The suggestion that every outgoing link weakens your own PR is an SEO myth. Outgoing links from your site that are thematically linked to your site's content actually help to reinforce the sense that your site is active in its particular area of expertise and therefore worth serving higher. Do not use this to overload every page on your website with links, thinking that it will help – each outgoing link you put in place has to be there for a reason and must enhance the content of your page, otherwise it is pointless.

Jargon buster

Reciprocal linking – The simple exchange of links between websites. A site agrees to place a link on one of its pages in exchange for a link from your site.

Themed linking – Sites similar in subject linking to each other. Also this can cover the internal linking of the pages in your site between each focused subject page – the use of plain html text linking between pages is recommended.

One-way linking – The formation of one way links using different methods.

Three-way linking – The formation of and understanding between two webmasters. Webmaster 'A' owns two sites (No.1 and No. 2). He links to your site from No.1, and in turn asks you to link to site No. 2.

Link farm – This is where your link is placed on many other sites, almost instantly. Normally a paid service, it is not in any theme and rarely results in any traffic. This is a misguided attempt to beat Google and the other major search engines. Not recommended!

Anchor text – The html text displayed and used in the link to your site eg: 'Click Here' – normally a blue underlined link.

Site-wide linking – This is where a webmaster agrees to place a link to your site on every page of his site.

Deep linking – The linking to internal pages of a site, normally aimed at a specific keyword and the page is normally in the same theme.

In content linking – Using articles with specific subjects and linking from those articles in the content to your site or in the form of a resource box at the end of the article.

8

Score your linking actions

Table 8.1 is handy guide that you can use to grade the effectiveness of your linking strategy. The far right column provides a grade that you should award yourself for each action you take. At the end of the table there is a score that tells you how effective your linking strategy is and what you should do to improve it further.

Table 8.1 A guide to grading the effectiveness of your linking strategy

What to pay attention to	What to do	Score
The anchor text of inbound links	As discussed earlier in this chapter, this is one of the most important factors for good rankings. It is best if you have a keyword in the anchor text, but, even if you don't, it is still OK.	+3
Origins of inbound links	Besides the anchor text, it is important that the site linking to you is a reputable one. Generally, sites with a greater Google PR are considered reputable.	+3
Links from similar sites	Having links from similar sites is very, very useful. It indicates that the competition is voting for you and you are popular within your topical community.	+3
Links from .edu and .gov sites	These links are precious because .edu and .gov sites are more reputable than .com. .biz, .info and such domains. Additionally, such links are hard to obtain.	+3
Number of back links	Generally, the more the better. The reputation of the sites that link to you is more important than their number, however. Also important is their anchor text – is there a keyword in it, how old are they, etc.	+3
The anchor text of internal links	This also matters, though not as much as the anchor text of inbound links.	+2
Around-the-anchor text	The text that is immediately before and after the anchor text also matters because it further indicates the relevance of the link – that is, if the link is artificial or naturally flows in the text.	+2
Age of inbound links	The older the better. Getting many new links in a short time suggests buying them.	+2

What to pay attention to	What to do	Score
Links from directories	These are great, though it strongly depends on which directories the links are from. Being listed in DMOZ, Yahoo! Directory and similar directories is a great boost for your ranking, but having tons of links from PR0 directories is useless and can even be regarded as link spamming if you have hundreds or thousands of such links.	+2
Number of outgoing links on the page that link to you	The fewer the better for you, as then your link looks more important.	+1
Named anchors	Named anchors (the target place of internal links) are useful for internal navigation, but also for SEO because you stress, additionally, that a particular page, paragraph or piece of text is important. In the code, named anchors look like this: `<A href= '#dogs'>Read about dogs</A>` The '#dogs' bit is the named anchor.	+1
IP address of inbound link	Google denies that it discriminates against links that come from the same IP address or C class of addresses, so, for Google, the IP address can be considered neutral in terms of the weight of inbound links. MSN and Yahoo!, however, may discard links from the same IPs or IP classes, so it is always better to get links from different IPs.	+1
Inbound links from link farms and other suspicious sites	This does not affect you in any way, provided that the links are not reciprocal. The idea is that it is beyond your control to define what a link farm links to, so you will not be penalised when such sites link to you because it is not your fault, but, in any case, you'd better stay away from link farms and similar suspicious sites.	0
Many outgoing links	Google does not like pages that consists mainly of links, so you're advised to keep the total to under 100 per page. Having many outgoing links does not confer any benefits in terms of ranking and could even make your situation worse.	−1

Score your linking actions (cont.)

What to pay attention to	What to do	Score
Excessive linking, link spamming	It is bad for your rankings when you have many links to/from the same sites (even if it is not a cross-linking scheme or links to bad neighbours) because it suggests link buying or at least spamming. In the best case, only some of the links are taken into account for SEO rankings.	−1
Outbound links to link farms and other suspicious sites	Unlike inbound links from link farms and other suspicious sites, outbound links to bad neighbours can drown you. Periodically, check the status of the sites you link to because sometimes good sites become bad neighbours and vice versa.	−3
Cross-linking	Cross-linking occurs when site A links to site B, site B links to site C and site A links back to site A. This is the simplest example, but more complex schemes are possible. Cross-linking looks like disguised reciprocal link trading and so it is penalised.	−3
Single pixel links	When you have a link that is a pixel or so wide, it is invisible to humans, so nobody will click on it. It is therefore, obvious that this link is an attempt to manipulate search engines.	−3

What your score means

- **22–26** Your linking strategy is generally very good, so maintain your efforts in exactly the same way that you have until now.

- **18–21** You need to develop your linking strategy, increasing the number of back links to your website and so on. You should also check your anchor text.

- **15–17** Your website is suffering from bad links and suspect linking strategies that are dragging it down. You need to work now to change that and increase its score.

- **Below 15** Your website has most probably been marked as a spam website. To change this you will need to increase the quality of your content, increase the number of back links and resubmit your website to the major search engines.

SEO and the social Web

9

Introduction

The social Web is now a fully integrated part of our online life. It is also an inescapable part of any kind of SEO you will undertake for your website. While most people think of Facebook when they think of the social Web (and rightly so), there are a lot more aspects to it than that and they are all vital to know.

In this chapter, we will look at what exactly the social Web is and how it can be employed in terms of SEO and online marketing. We will see why it is important and how you can best use it in the SEO efforts you employ for your website.

What you'll do

Learn what social marketing is

Find out about the social marketing channels on the Web

Learn why the social Web is important to your SEO

Set up a Facebook page for your website

Set up a Myspace profile for your website

Set up an Orkut profile for your website

Learn about Twitter and Tumblr

Use a Tumblr account

Set up a Twitter account

Link up your social profiles

What is social marketing?

Social marketing was 'born' as a discipline in the 1970s, when Philip Kotler and Gerald Zaltman realised that the same marketing principles being used to sell *products* to consumers could be used to 'sell' ideas, attitudes and behaviours. Kotler and Alan Andreasen define social marketing (Andreasen, *Social Marketing in the 21st Century*, Sage, 2006, p. 65) as:

> *differing from other areas of marketing only with respect to the objectives of the marketer and his or her organisation. Social marketing seeks to influence social behaviours not to benefit the marketer, but to benefit the target audience and the general society.*

Today, commonly, the idea of what social marketing is, at a superficial level, has become (depending on who you ask):

> online marketing using Facebook and any of the online social networks.

Yet, the underlying philosophy of the original concept – taking marketing from being something designed to help the one doing the *selling* to something designed to help the one doing the *buying* – is still the guiding principle of social marketing.

When it comes to enhancing your website's SEO status, the change that occurs the moment the social marketing component is added is it turns from being online marketing designed to benefit your website into online marketing designed to add real value to the Web and its content.

Myspace

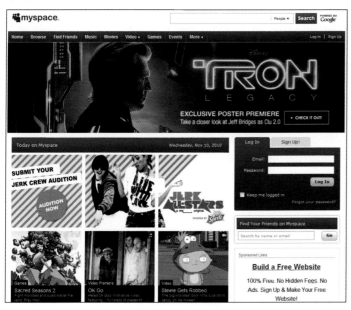

Myspace (at: **www.myspace.com**) used to be the daddy of this genre – no other site had received as much publicity as Myspace had. It was like the Oracle of data storage or the Cisco of network devices. As such, it has both ardent fans as well as vitriolic critics.

It was originally started by Tom Andersen and Chris DeWolfe in November 2003 (though there is some dispute as to what it should be for – data storage or a community) and acquired by Rupert Murdoch's News Corporation in July 2005 for $580 million.

As a social networking site, Myspace is a one-stop shop. You can add pictures, write blogs, make friends, upload music and videos, organise offline events with your online buddies and do gazillions of other things (shave Britney and get a ringtone). Myspace's USP is that, unlike most other social networking sites, it offers you complete leeway to modify and customise your profile page. You get to decide which colours and fonts to keep, what apps to embed and what the look and feel of your profile should be. These effects are achieved by copying and pasting simple HTML and CSS code, using the Myspace Profile Editor, but the results are good.

The social marketing channels on the Web (cont.)

Eight rules for that perfect social network profile picture

1. Have a professional or a dedicated amateur take your picture.

2. Use a white background, or at least a neutral one. No trees! No snowstorms!

3. The idea of having your significant other in the picture is a good one, at least in terms of maintaining peace in the presence of a jealous or nervous spouse. But people are not friending your partner, they are friending you. I'd vote for the picture to be solo.

4. If you are wearing a hat, you better have both a good reason and a good hat.

5. I totally understand that you are shy, modest and self-effacing. But sabotaging your photo is not a good way to communicate that. We just assume you're a dork.

6. Conceptual photos (your foot, a monkey wearing glasses) may give us insight into the real you, but perhaps you could save that insight for the second impression.

Once you have tweaked your profile to your heart's content, it's time to get cracking. Whenever a new account is opened, Tom Andersen (the founder) is added to the friends list by default. As he remains a friend in the majority of the lists, this is a place to start hunting for friends in case you don't know anybody at Myspace. Of course, you can idly browse through profiles from the main page and latch on to somebody interesting. If you have friends already, then it's a walk in the park. As you start developing your contacts and making new friends, though, you will find that your world revolves around it.

Communication is via the usual suspects – messages, bulletins and IMs. The groups section is a hot and happening place where people gather together based on their interests and talk – the same goes for the forum area.

Events are things happening in real life – from a rock concert to a picnic – that are either featured on the site or can be organised by you. Myspace also has separate featured areas for filmmakers, musicians and comedians. In fact, to add music to your profile, all you have to do is go to Myspace Music and select music from there. It might sound restrictive but you have got almost every band and artist there is to choose from. For videos, you have a little more freedom. At Myspace TV, you still have to select from the featured videos in different categories – comedy, sport, entertainment and so on – but if you are hot on a video, you can submit its link for it to be considered for featuring. Classifieds and jobs are also useful areas of the site.

Myspace, as mentioned, has a lot of detractors as well as fans, and most of them have a valid point or two. As far as the site's design goes, the 'anything goes' philosophy followed by the users while designing their profiles is reported to cause problems, from messed-up views to browser freezes to music and videos starting up simultaneously. Even more serious are reports that Myspace is a haven for phishers and spyware. Safety for underage users also remains a concern, with online predators using devious means to contact young people. In fact, Myspace does not conform to W3C standards of valid HTML usage.

Orkut

Ask the GenNext in India which site they visit when they connect to the Internet and 90 per cent would answer, 'Orkut'. Orkut's (at: **www.orkut.com**) popularity in places such as India and Brazil (most Orkut users are Brazilians) and its anonymity in the USA (where it is domiciled) is a mystifying puzzle that seems to obey the law of unintended consequences (a good doctoral thesis topic for sociologists).

Orkut was launched on 17 November 2002 by Google. It was the brainchild of Orkut Büyükkökten, a Turkish software engineer who developed it as an independent project while working at Google.

Orkut was launched keeping the US market in view, but the service actually found its feet in Brazil, where the name 'Orkut' has ingrained itself into the national consciousness. In fact Brazilians, and to some degree Asians such as Indians and Pakistanis, are huge fans of Orkut. In its *intended* market, Orkut is overshadowed by similar sites, such as Myspace and Facebook. The top three for Orkut by demographics, though, are Brazil (56 per cent), USA (19 per cent) and India (15 per cent), while visits countrywise are Brazil (72.5 per cent),

7 How beautiful you are is a distant second to how happy you are. In my experience, photos that communicate openness and enthusiasm are far more appealing than photos that make you look like a supermodel.

8 Cropping is so important. A well cropped photo sends a huge, subliminal message to other people. If you don't know how to do this, browse through the work of professionals and see how they do it. It matters.

9

The social marketing channels on the Web (cont.)

India (16.1 per cent) and USA (2.7 per cent). This second bit of data is more reliable than the first because users can put any country as their place of birth or residence.

The features available on Orkut are no doubt known to most, but for those who came in late, Orkut offers a very friendly and uncluttered interface in the tradition of Google. In fact, unlike Myspace, there is no provision to customise your profile. Even though it seems a little monotonous, the eye sometimes yearns for uniformity, so Orkut's interface is both its biggest advantage as well as its disadvantage. People can be added to your friends list simply by clicking **Add as friend** tab in their profiles, though the request has to be accepted. People can be banned by adding them to an **Ignore** list. Then there is stuff such as the Fans and Crush list, which are great to dabble in when you are tired of twiddling your thumbs.

Members can communicate via scraps – think of them as like writing e-mails without having to fill in all those pesky details. The scraps are publicly viewable. There is also a privately viewable Message option, but it is rarely used.

People come together in groups, which are called Communities. Each Community has an owner and may have a moderator and are grouped by common interest. Polls were introduced in 2007 for every community. Apart from polls, Google has introduced a slew of new features, but the Profile album was there from the start. You could always upload maximum of 12 photos with optional captions, but, now that Google has acquired YouTube, it has become possible to upload videos from YouTube or Google video by attaching the link. The video plays inline.

Google Talk can also be launched from within Orkut and the online status of your Google Talk's contacts can be known in real time, if both they and you have signed in using Google accounts. Profile views since February 2006 (the numbers tend to massage your ego), as well as the names of the five most recent profile visitors, are displayed. Two brand new features – RSS feeds for your blogs, as well as Orkut's very own blog, open to all users – are going to warm the cockles of the hearts of avid bloggers.

Orkut has had its fair share of controversies, too. It has been banned in Saudi Arabia and Iran. In India, Orkut has been the target of political parties, such as the Shiv Sena, and also come under the scrutiny of the courts for featuring anti-India communities. In Brazil, charges of the propagation of racism by users have hit the portal.

Although it would appear that, in terms of social marketing, Orkut is probably, for UK users, a last-minute consideration, the very fact that it is a Google property makes it a must-use social network. Content posted on it (as we shall see) is indexed fast and helps to promote your website, so it is vital that you do not overlook it.

Facebook

Unless you have been living in a barrel at the bottom of the sea, you will not have failed to hear about Facebook and its massive potential for marketing and SEO. With over 500 million users worldwide, Facebook (at: **www.facebook.com**) has become the behemoth of social marketing networks and the one on which everyone focuses as a matter of course.

It is usually mentioned first, but I have included it here last, not because I do not think it is important, but because it is wrong to allow its size to dictate its importance. In terms of SEO, to us, Facebook is equally as important as the previous two social networks we have been looking at here and the principles that guide our online activities in it are exactly the same.

9

Why is the social Web important to your SEO?

▶

SEO is about making your website visible. I can get very technical here or we can use the example of a party. Imagine a very crowded party where you, just another guest, will play the role of a search engine and the website you are looking for will be one of the guests. In order to help make it easier to find the guest, he is wearing a red shirt.

In a party where there are hundreds of guests, music, waiters and so on in a sprawling mansion, finding that single guest, despite his bright red shirt (which is his SEO efforts), is very hard. You will spend time walking around, looking for him, but, as nothing stands still at a party (or indeed online), you can never be sure where he is or even if he is actually at the party.

Now suppose that this guest you are looking for is not only wearing a red shirt but a red shirt made of a particular rare fabric with a very distinct monogram on the breast pocket. Both the fabric and the monogram are so unique that they are a talking point wherever he goes.

This means that the guest is now leaving a trail of impressions for you to find. As you wander around the crowded, noisy, ever-changing landscape of this party looking for this elusive guest, you will find a trail of anecdotes and the people you meet can guide you to where they saw him last.

Someone, for instance, says she thought he was by the bar and someone else that he saw him go upstairs and, once you go upstairs, someone else says, yes, the man you are looking for is out on the first-floor balcony, admiring the swimming pool below.

Now, the guest in the red shirt became infinitely easier to find once he left a social network trail that you, the search engine, could follow. Further, not only are you now *able* to track him down but you are also likely be impressed by his importance and probably beginning to think that this person, who appears to be so popular, will be likeable even though you have not yet met him.

This, slightly corny, example shows exactly why social Web marketing is important for your website's standing with search engines.

facebook

Email
paul@webdirectstudio.com
☑ Keep me logged in

Password
••••••••
Forgot your password?

Login

Create a Page

Community Page

Generate support for your favorite cause or topic by creating a Community Page. If it becomes very popular (attracting thousands of fans), it will be adopted and maintained by the Facebook community. Learn more.

Please note that you will not be able to edit the name of a Page after it has been created.

Page name:

(examples: Elect Jane Smith, Recycling)

Create Community Page

Official Page

Communicate with your customers and fans by creating and maintaining an official Facebook Page.

Please note that you will not be able to edit the name of a Page after it has been created.

Create a Page for a:

○ Local business
○ Brand, product, or organization
○ Artist, band, or public figure

Page name:

(examples: Summer Sky Cafe, Springfield Jazz Trio)

☐ I'm the official representative of this person, business, band or product and have permission to create this Page. Review the Facebook Terms

Create Official Page

Facebook © 2010 · English (US)

Mobile · Find Friends · Badges · About · Advertising · Developers · Careers · Privacy · Terms · Help

2

💡

Jargon buster

Wall – the common jargon on Facebook. Wall is a space on each users profile page where other friends can post messages. One user's wall is visible to anyone. Wall is just a public message to a user on Facebook

Poke – a poke is well discussed feature on Facebook. If you don't have anything to say but just want to make your friend aware that 'I am here' you can use poke, Poke can be interpreted in their own ways. It is just a flirting on Facebook

Events – used to let your friends know about upcoming events in their community and helps to organize social gatherings.

Status – you can micro-blog using this feature. With this you can inform your friends about your current actions, thoughts etc.

◀ # Setting up a Facebook page for your website

1 Create a special, unique e-mail address for your website's page only. If you set up the page properly, you can change it later if you need to (note that the name of a Community Page cannot be changed, though, unless you have fewer than 100 followers). It does have to be an e-mail address that actually exists and you (or whomever the FB Page administrator will be) can actually access. Ideally, auto-forward the e-mail address to the FB Page Administrator's primary e-mail address.

2 Log out of Facebook. Go to **www.facebook.com** and, in the **Official Page, Create a Page for a:** section, click **Local business, Brand, Product, or organisation** or **Artist, band, or public figure**. Alternatively, go to **www. facebook.com/pages/create. php** directly. (Go with the Official Page option – ignore **Community Page** for now).

9

Setting up a
Facebook page
for your website
(cont.)

3 Use the unique e-mail address you previously set up as the basis for the business account you're creating to set up the page and populate it with your personal information (birthday and so on). That can be changed later at any stage.

4 Activate the account and set up the page. Add your personal account and any other accounts necessary as additional admins. Go to **Edit the Page**, look at the lower right-hand column for **Admins** and click **Add**. You'll have to choose the **Add by email** option as your newly created business account will have no friends. There you have it.

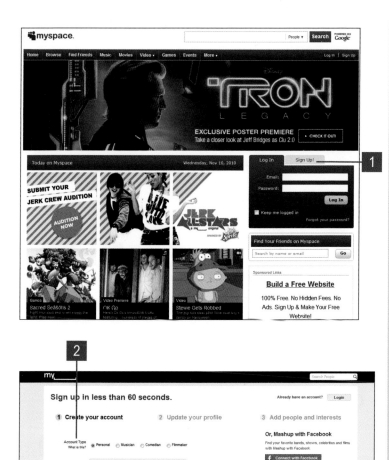

Setting up a Myspace profile for your website

1 To do this, you first need to sign up. Go to **www.myspace. com** and simply click **Sign Up** on the homepage and then complete the **Sign up for Myspace** form that appears.

2 Pay close attention to the fact that if you are a musician, filmmaker or comedian, Myspace has special profiles you can take advantage of in the **Account Type** section of the above form.

3 After you have signed up, you will be asked to post a photo of yourself. If you want to do so, click the **Browse** tab, find your photo on your computer, then click **Upload**. If you don't want to add a photo to your Myspace account, click **Skip for now**. You can always add your photo later if you want to.

4 The next page allows you to send e-mails to all your friends so that they can sign up to Myspace, too. If they already have a Myspace account, they will be added to your friends list. If you don't want to sign up any friends right now, click **Skip for now**.

5 That's it! All done.

SEO and the social Web 157

Setting up an Orkut profile for your website

1 Go to **www.orkut.com** and sign up using your Google Account login and password, if you have set this up. If you do not have a Google Account, click **Create an account**.

2 To get the most out of Orkut and to have more friends, you'll need to complete the personal details in your profile by following the next couple of steps.

3 Visit your homepage and click the **settings** tab at the top.

4 Fill in all the relevant information on the **Profile** tab, without neglecting the **Privacy**, **General**, **Notification** and **Updates** ones, then click **Save**, bottom left

5 That's it. You're set!

No chapter on the social Web would ever be complete without mentioning Twitter (**http://twitter.com**) and Tumblr (**www.tumblr.com**).

In many ways, these two are complementary – one filling in for the limitations of the other.

Twitter is a micro-blogging service where messages are posted to an online community. This community looks set to go past the 1 billion members mark in a couple of years. Tumblr is an oddity. It has the immediacy of a micro-blogging service, like Twitter, but the capabilities of a traditional blog. This means that it inhabits a middle ground between the micro-blogging and macro-blogging platforms.

Right now, of the two, only Tumblr is important to us here because of its ability to provide a handy connecting service between social networks that's hassle-free, easy to use and free.

One of the biggest of the factors that have added to the success of Tumblr (**www.tumblr.com**) is its simple registration form. It is not at all a time-consuming task, which caters perfectly for the psychology of Internet surfers. Researches have proved that people who surf the Net are very impatient. So, Tumblr's registration form has purposely been kept very easy. Users only have to fill in the urgently required fields.

Twitter and Tumblr

See also

Twitter and Tumblr are both covered further in Chapter 10, where the real-time Web and its implications for SEO are discussed.

9

Email address

Password

URL *(you can change this at any time)*

.tumblr.com

Sign up and start posting!

Twitter and Tumblr (cont.)

Officially founded by David Karp, Tumblr is the product of the multimedia blogs hand-coded by a bunch of innovative bloggers who did not restrict themselves to any preconceptions about blogging formats. That is why it is more like reading a tweet than a fully fledged conventional blog.

The times and this kind of platform are witnessing rapid change and Tumblr is the product of the founders having availed themselves of the best possible tools for blogging. The content types have a variety of built-in formats that makes Tumblr stand apart from the other available blogging platforms. There are several templates that have been pooled by a variety of creative talents. With the help of Tumblr, it actually becomes very easy to stylise your blog and the whys and hows of design are made very accessible.

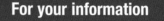

For your information

When microblogging, make every word count, get to know your readers, revolutionise the art of link sharing and write fearlessly. Here's how:

Practice the art of economical expression. Microblogging is all about brevity. Twitter restricts each tweet to 140 characters, and while there's no limit on Tumblr, it's against the spirit of the service to be too verbose. As bloggers, we're often told to omit unnecessary words and to leave out the parts that people skip. Microblogging is the perfect medium to help you hone this useful skill.

Keep your finger on the pulse. Twitter, especially, is useful for this. It's become something of a social bookmarking service, with users sharing links to interesting articles or breaking news. It's a useful place not only to find great links but to gauge what people are talking about at the moment, all great fodder for blog posts.

Develop the skill of writing now, worrying later. Microblogging is casual. It's not your magnum opus, so typos and errors in expression don't matter. It's the perfect platform to practice free writing without constantly stopping to critique your words.

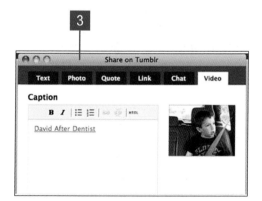

Add a Link

Title *(optional)*

URL

Add a description

✔ Create post   Preview   Cancel

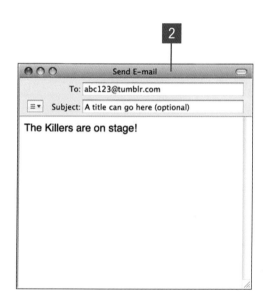

Using a Tumblr account

1 To use this amazing social networking platform once you have signed up, you just need to drop the URL in the **Add a Link** area and you are ready to get set, go with anything you want to add and share in your network.

2 Blogging is not a problem because it is loaded with HTML and a WYSIWYG editor. You can post via e-mails, an iPhone application, AIM and many others on Tumblr.

3 Unlike Facebook, which only allows you to track people in your network, Tumblr, just like Twitter, offers a wide scope for connectivity. You cannot only share information with your friends but also with people of similar interests and experience, which opens up a totally dynamic and new world of shared posts and experiences.

9

Using a Tumblr account (cont.)

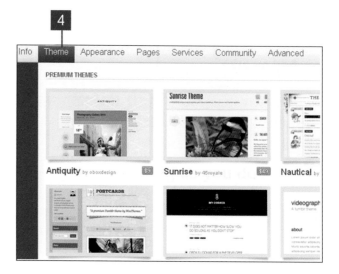

4 You can have complete control over your blog and set up a group with multiple authors. Tumblr makes it a simple task to set up a number of blogs under the shade of a single account. You can select the option to customise your Tumblr blog. Then, you can change the theme and opt for one among lots of available themes. Also, you can change the appearance of the page by changing the fonts and so on. You can even add cascading style sheets (CSS) to set the look and navigation controls for your blog.

5 Also, it gives you the privilege of keeping your password-protected blogs and allows you the control to share with a particular set of people or other group of your choice.

6 It helps users to discover a new set of interesting content, including graphics, pictures, videos or links, with the help of Tumblr's popular 'What's new' section and even *The Wire*.

Once you have a profile on Tumblr you will be almost ready to see just how to save time. You just need to do one more thing – a necessity anyway – that is, set up a Twitter account (if you have not got one already).

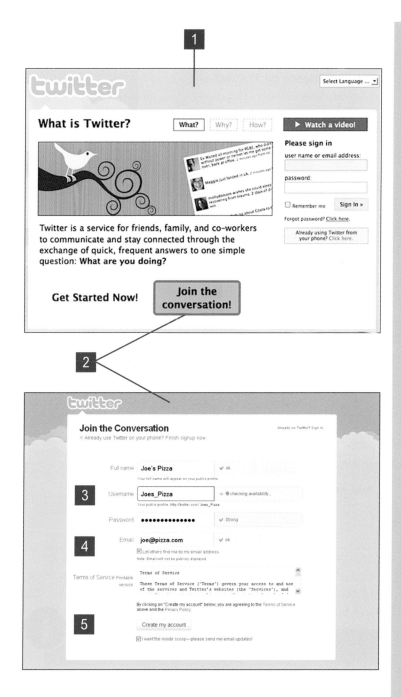

Setting up a Twitter account

1 Go to **http://twitter.com**. You'll see this screen.

2 Click **Join the conversation!** and this screen will appear.

3 To create your account you need to enter a username. If you are using this Twitter account for brand management for your business, I'd recommend using your domain name minus the dot com/net/ and so on (**http://twitter. com/mymarketingname**, for example). If it's just for fun or personal use, use whatever you want as the username.

4 Add your e-mail address – personal or business.

5 Type in the words you see, which are for security, then click **I accept, Create my account** (if you want, you can read the Terms of Service too).

9

Setting up a Twitter account (cont.)

6 Start connecting! As you can see, Twitter asks for your e-mail information to check if anyone you know is on Twitter. Click **continue** once you've entered your e-mail address and password.

7 Here's what the next page looks like. You can now handpick which of your new Twitter friends you want to add from those listed.

8 There's also an option to invite non-Twitter users to set up Twitter accounts. If you plan to use Twitter for business and you already have a pretty big database of names and email address, this could be a great opportunity to show your clients you care by connecting with them in a new way. Twitter can be a great way to communicate and deal with customer care issues, too!

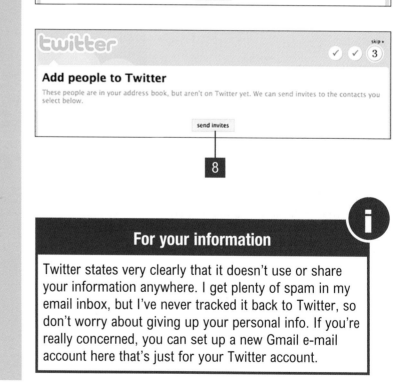

Are your friends on Twitter?

We can check if anyone in your email contacts already has a Twitter account.

Search Web Email (Hotmail, Yahoo, Gmail, Etc.)

Your Email [ ] @ Gmail ▾

Email Password [ ]

🔒 **Email Security**
We don't store your login, your password is submitted securely, and we don't email without your permission.

continue »

skip »

6

7

38 people from your address book are using Twitter!

Select the people you'd like to start following.

continue »

Add people to Twitter

These people are in your address book, but aren't on Twitter yet. We can send invites to the contacts you select below.

send invites

8

For your information

Twitter states very clearly that it doesn't use or share your information anywhere. I get plenty of spam in my email inbox, but I've never tracked it back to Twitter, so don't worry about giving up your personal info. If you're really concerned, you can set up a new Gmail e-mail account here that's just for your Twitter account.

For your information

Twitter's popularity means that it now has its own 'language'.

Following
The term for 'friending' on Twitter. When you follow someone, their tweets will show up in the feed on your Twitter homepage. When someone follows you, your tweets will show up in the feed on their Twitter homepage. Following does not have to be reciprocal, someone can follow you without you following them back, and vice versa. Your Twitter homepage will give you a count of the number of people you are following and the number that are following you.

About Twitter's Follow Friday
It is a Twitter social convention where you Tweet the names of Twitter users you'd like others to follow and hashtag it with #followfriday or #ff. The concept can be compared attending a school pep rally and receiving a public 'attaboy' from a well-liked peer. It's a compliment to someone to have you recommend them by their Twitter name on Follow Friday (more about hashtags below).

Tweets/Tweeting
When you speak to all your followers by typing news, links or other information into your status update bar. These tweets can also be seen by people who aren't your followers and even by people who don't have a Twitter account. Keep in mind there is no built in spell check and no deleting. The limit is 140 characters including spaces.

Defining Retweets (RTs)
This is when you repost something someone else has said so that your followers see it. Do this by typing the letters RT, then space, then @username, then copying their tweet in its entirety including the odd looking link at the end. This is considered a huge compliment in the Twitter World. You can also add your own opinion (e.g. 'funny' or 'well written') if there is space. The total number of characters allowed remains 140.

9

Linking up your social profiles ▶

Now that you have set up your Tumblr and Twitter accounts, you are ready to turn your efforts into a social media marketing and SEO online force by linking everything together.

While it's cool to have multiple social network accounts and work them so that they begin to have an impact on your website's online presence, they all require the one thing you do not have a lot of – time.

In this section you will see just how you can free up time by doing more than one social network activity at a time.

1 Link up your Facebook account by, first, logging on to your Facebook account.

2 Once you are on your profile page, copy the URL **www. facebook.com/apps/application. php?id=2231777543** and paste it in the address window of your browser. This will take you to the next screen where you will be able to see the Facebook Twitter application that will enable you to link the two accounts. Click **Go to Application**.

3 You should now see the following screen. Input your Twitter username and password in the box that appears, then click **Allow** to authorise Twitter to link to your Facebook page.

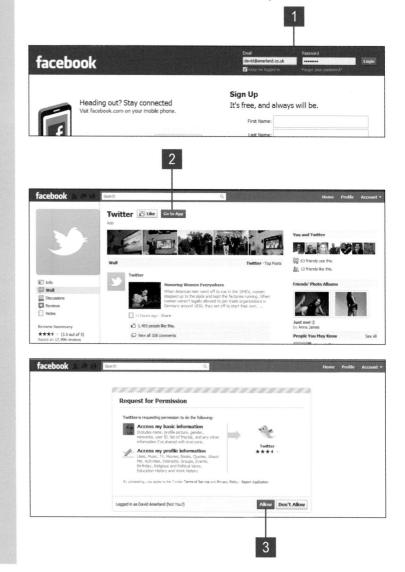

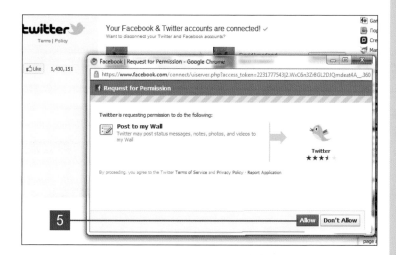

4 When the linking has been completed you will see this screen. Under **Allow Twitter to post updates to:**, tick **Facebook Profile**.

5 You will now see this screen. Click **Allow**. When the cross-linking process has been completed, the box you ticked to allow Twitter to post updates to your Facebook profile will remain ticked.

6 Next, under **Allow Twitter to post updates to:**, tick **Facebook Page**.

7 Choose the Facebook page you want to link up, then click **Allow** on the permission pop-up box that will appear and you are all set. If you have more than one Facebook page set up, you will need to repeat the process for each one in turn until they are all linked up.

8 Once you have done this, you're all done. Now each time you post a Tweet, your Facebook wall on your main Facebook profile and your Facebook pages will be updated automatically.

9

Linking up your social profiles (cont.)

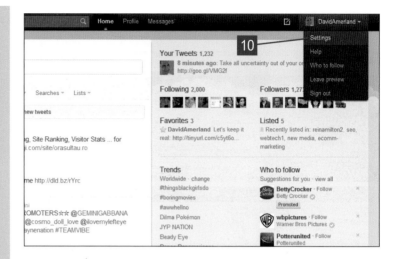

9 Now, link your Twitter account by logging in using your username and password.

10 At the top right-hand side, you will see your username. Click on that and, in the dropdown menu, choose **Settings**.

11 On the next screen, click **Connections**. This screen allows you to manage all the applications that cross-talk to your Twitter profile from your social network profiles.

12 You are almost there! Just two more steps to go. The first of these is at Myspace (**www.myspace.com**)

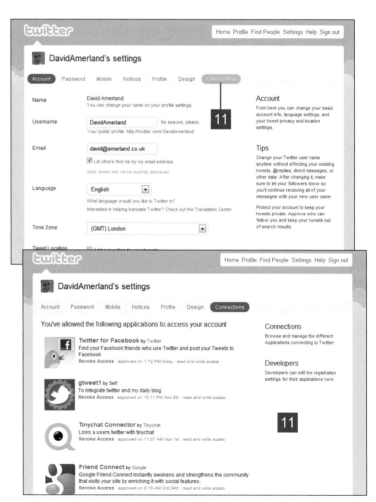

13

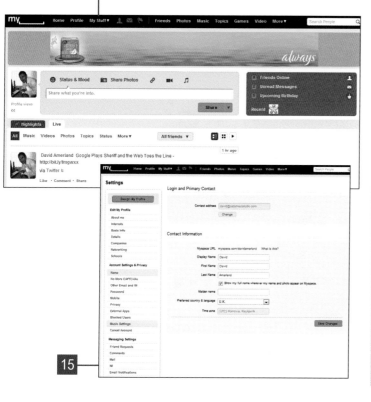

14

15

Linking up your social profiles (cont.)

13 Log in on the homepage using your username and password.

14 On the next screen, click **My Stuff** at the top right-hand side.

15 Click on **Stream sync settings**.

9

Linking up your social profiles (cont.)

16 You will now see the three main services that you can sync your Myspace page to – Twitter, Facebook and YouTube. Click **Get Synced** next to each service.

17 Each time you click, you will be taken to the login screen for the service, where you will have to input your username and password, when you've done that click **Allow** and the syncing will occur.

18 When you choose to allow syncing to occur, you will be directed back to Myspace, where you will need to make one more selection to allow the sync to be bidirectional. Then, whatever you post on Myspace, for instance, will also become visible on Twitter and Facebook and vice versa.

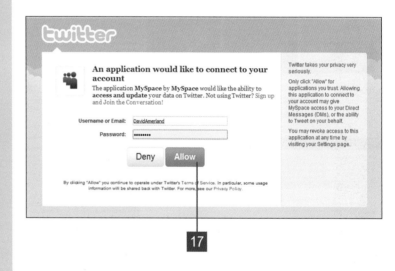

Linking up your social profiles (cont.)

19 Confirmation that this process has worked successfully can be seen in the next screen.

20 The final stage of this interlinking involves Tumblr. Go to **www.tumblr.com** and log in using your username and password. Once logged in to your account, click **Goodies** at the top.

21 You will now see all the applications available to you to help you sync accounts. We are primarily interested in two, here: the one that syncs Tumblr and Twitter and the one which syncs Tumblr and Facebook.

22 Click the Facebook one first. The application will install automatically and you should then be taken to your Facebook account, if you are still logged on – otherwise, you will asked to log in first. You will see that posts made on Tumblr are automatically imported to your Facebook wall posts feed.

Linking up your social profiles (cont.)

23 When you have done that, go back to Tumblr, click **Goodies** again and, this time, click the Twitter sync application.

24 On the next screen, you will need to make sure that **Send my Tumblr posts to Twitter** is ticked.

25 Then, click **SAVE + CLOSE** at the top right-hand side.

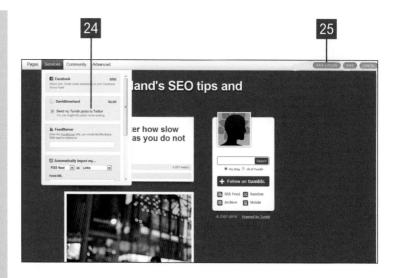

That's it! You have now successfully created a powerful, interlinked online presence for your website. Each time you post new content or bring in a new product, you should mention it on Tumblr, which is linked to Twitter, which is linked to Facebook and Myspace. In this way you will have managed, in a relatively easy way, to work all your major social network accounts at once!

There is an additional benefit to this because, by being active in this fashion, on the social Web, you are not just benefiting your SEO but also increasing your presence on the real-time Web. This is the latest development on the Web and, befittingly, it is the subject of the next, final chapter of this book.

SEO and the real-time Web

Introduction

The real-time Web is the latest trend in a series of trends that are closely linked to the development of the Web in terms of size, and its technologies in terms of capabilities. The real-time Web takes SEO and turns it into marketing and vice versa. It does this as a result of its ability to increase the visibility of websites.

In many ways, this has been an inevitable and, perhaps, entirely predictable development. The 'right offer, right time, right marketing channel' mantra of the 1990s has met the Internet and created a 'best of both worlds' solution labelled real-time marketing.

In this chapter we shall see what real-time marketing is, what the channels of the real-time Web are and how you can best use it all to help your site be found more easily and become more successful.

What you'll do

Find out what the real-time Web is

See why the real-time Web is important

Find out what Web 2.5 is and how it will affect your SEO efforts

Read about the future of the real-time Web

Set up an RSS feed to help promote your website

Activate FeedBurner's SmartFeed

Integrate your FeedBurner feed into your blog platform

What is the real-time Web?

If we accept the technical definition of it, the real-time Web is a set of technologies and practices that enable users to receive information as soon as it is published by its authors, rather than requiring that they or their software check a source periodically for updates.

In other words, the real-time Web is the digital equivalent of the offline world where things, in order to happen, require an immediate interaction and some kind of transactional value in the exchange of data. Luckily for you, as you have followed the steps given in Chapter 9 and created accounts on Twitter and Tumblr, you have already taken the first step onto the real-time Web.

For your information

Social Web: While there is still a lot of maturing to do on the enterprise side, consumers are leading the charge in establishing the social Web as a primary component of marketing.

Mobile Web: The mobile Web has grown at a stunning pace in the last 5 years and continues to break new ground. Much of the excitement has been focused on the iPhone, but there are other trends that are having a real impact. Mobile is driving much of the consumerisation of IT, and mobile apps continue to be a foothold for more creative uses of the Web by enterprise IT.

Real-time Web: Until now the concept of the real-time Web has been relegated to being a euphemism for the rapid delivery of data streams to the end user. 'Real-time search', for example, is focused on delivering the same search results more rapidly.

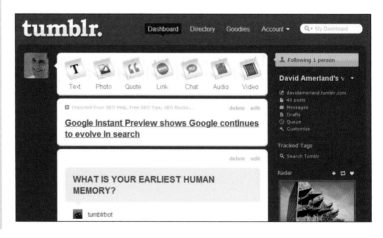

It used to be that news was not news until it happened on TV. There is a degree of truth to this that is hard to argue against once you start to analyse the way in which we consider news to be news and it is the same with Google and the 'arrival' of anything. That is exactly what makes Google so powerful.

The ubiquitous presence of the search engines and their ability to index the Web gives them the power to make something 'exist' or not, as far as users are concerned. The real-time Web is a phenomenon that has grown out of the increased interactivity of Web pages and the explosive interest in and popularity of social network sites such as Facebook and micro-blogging services of the likes of Twitter.

With news and data spread more and more through these sites than Google itself, it was only a matter of time before the Google search, with its old-fashioned, traditional sequential, top-down approach, would change.

Caffeine is Google's latest search algorithm. It is a radical departure from the old model in that it takes into account the full multimedia, multi-Web point presence of a website and serves search query results in ways that are designed to be more sensitive to:

- content
- context
- geo-location
- trends
- brand
- multimedia.

The ultimate result of this, in plain English, is that, as a webmaster, you now need to be truly versed in the use of the social Web, networking your website as well as producing content for it and promoting it to search engines. On the upside, the sensitivity of Google to the real-time Web means that content posted on sites being worked properly will be indexed much faster than before and that is, obviously, very good news indeed.

What is the real-time Web? (cont.)

Jargon buster

Real-time Web – A set of technologies and practices that enable users to receive information as soon as it is published by its authors, rather than requiring that they or their software check a source periodically for updates. As such specific website technologies become part of it: the RSS feed of a website, for instance, the Newstream of Facebook and, obviously, any micro-blogging platform.

10

Why is the real-time Web important?

▶

The real-time Web is important because its trends and development always affect the way you SEO your website. While it has little to do with SEO per se, it does help increase the visibility of websites and it does affect end users' (what we call online visitors) behaviour.

To make the point clearer, I will provide two small examples, one of which is metaphorical and the other is real.

First, the metaphor. Let's say that you are invited to a carnival. It is a large, colourful, ever more energetic gathering that appears (from afar) to be just at the edge of getting out of control. It is held on a long street with several sidestreets. You will play the role of a search engine. Another carnival goer, attired in a colourful costume will play the role of a website. Your mission is to find the website – after all, those tall feathers on her head should make her conspicuous.

The carnival is large and ever evolving and ever changing, in terms of the cohesion of the shape and social groups there. You trawl around, looking for the lady with the feathers, but, as you ask other people and peer down the sidestreets, she appears all the more elusive. Someone tells you, for instance, that she is on a certain road, while someone else tells you she is on a float. The more you ask, the more confused you become and the lady flits about, evading your attention.

Now suppose the lady, instead of silently flitting along like a ghost, is actually a gregarious, outgoing person who simply charms everyone she meets. Now your task of finding her has become a whole lot easier. On the way to the bar sidestreet, where she was last seen, you meet someone else who tells you that they have just seen her on a certain float and, as you get there, you find at least three people who can confirm where she is going to go next. Your task has been made so much easier simply because she has interacted socially.

Now remember that you are the search engine and the lady with the feathers is a website you are looking to find. The example, I hope, helps you to visualise why the real-time Web is important to your website's visibility.

My next example is a lot more practical and much shorter.

Google, very recently, introduced an additional feature to its search called Google Instant. This feature is intended to help those looking for something save a little bit of time (half a second or so, according to studies) by checking what they are typing in the Google search box and making suggestions based on popular, similar searches.

In order to achieve this, Google automatically (and incredibly fast) checks its records of similar searches by tens of thousands of other users and makes suggestions. The intention (by Google) is good, but, by helping online visitors in this way, it skews the search results towards popular searches drawn from the popularity of some search terms.

This means that the SEO of your website for a particular niche must now also take into account the suggestions given by Google Instant in order to benefit from the traffic they could bring.

While Google Instant is not a change in terms of how a search works, it perfectly showcases the way *cosmetic* changes on the Web can affect your SEO.

Which is why the real-time Web is important to your website.

10

What is Web 2.5 and how will it affect your SEO efforts?

If you are new to the concept of Web 2.0, then Web 2.5 is going to seem like a step too far, so there is a need here to recap, briefly, and explain just what is going on.

When the term Web 2.0 came on the scene at a Web summit conference in 2005 as a marketing ploy that was too good a soundbite *not* to use, there was no agreement on what it meant or if there was, even, a Web 1.0 concept.

The Web, of course, is evolutionary in nature and capabilities, so it makes sense to think of it as versions. It would appear a moot point, therefore, to wonder whether or not there is any sense in giving it version numbers. The very fact that this has become widespread in marketing terms means that now the term has acquired a meaning and has become a means of pushing further development.

In view of this, Web 1.0 was a passive repository of information. Think of it like a library. In the early days of the Web, information existed to be accessed, but was hard to find. Then, once you *did* find it, all you could do was consume it.

What Web 2.0 stands for is interactivity. Suddenly, Web platforms started to change from passive to interactive. They allowed users to leave comments, vote for files or pages, access downloadable material, create accounts and limited online profiles. If Web 1.0 was the establishment of websites and online platforms of information, Web 2.0 was the opening up of the doors of the library and the moment the crowd was allowed in.

This has led to the development of interactive Web platforms that allow the visitor to either contribute to their content in a limited way or leave a trace of their presence there. Web 2.0 has been a much friendlier place and has led to more online visitor interaction, which, in turn, has led to more interactive platforms and, before we knew, it became transformed into the place we all hang out in after work and before sleep.

Web 2.0, then, started out as interaction. Its defining characteristic (if it could be said to have a single one) was the fact that, suddenly, capabilities were being added to websites and online presences so that, slowly, a degree of personalisation started to take place. Online users also started to *add* information as well as just retrieve it. Blogs, comments, forum posts, videos and audio files all played a part in this.

During all this change, SEO remained an arcane science, little understood by many. Webmasters thought that it was the work of web designers to know it and Web designers thought it was something coders should do. Coders, though, did not know who to turn to and hardly anyone really understood what search engine optimisers did.

The reliance on search engines to find information, however – itself a significant characteristic of Web 2.0 development – led to an increase in the visibility of SEO and those who practise it and a clearer understanding of its importance.

The Web 2.5 era is now upon us. Web platforms have become more and more interactive, the social Web and the real-time Web are now part of our daily routine and information is collaborative, in the sense that it is used, created, consumed and spread via a complex online social Web model mirroring the complexity and interactions happening in the offline world.

In terms of SEO and the visibility of your website, the Web is now so crowded and so large that to have a Web presence without a coherent SEO strategy in place is akin to driving with one arm tied behind your back. It can be done, but it is less than ideal and may contribute to a crash rather than end with you getting to your destination.

Web 2.5 is the next natural step towards using the collective information we have created and its main aim is deep interaction and the ability to harness intelligence. Onsite search, engines and subscription tools, Google alerts and a more sensitive search, plus the immediacy of the real-time Web, characterise a stage of Web development where SEO alone, in terms of optimising a website, is no longer enough.

It is pointless, for instance, to have your website optimised to the gills and appearing high on search engines when your target customers are to be found mostly on a number of social network sites and have little extra time to use search engines to look for our website. It is also pointless to think about onpage SEO when you also need to have multiple presences on the Web in terms of Facebook, Twitter, articles, PRs and profile pages elsewhere.

In the era of Web 2.5, the choices are simple: increase your site's interactivity, increase its online presence and learn to fish where the fish are – the days of customers coming to *you* are simply gone.

10

The future of the real-time Web

We have been discussing cutting-edge issues regarding the way the real-time Web might affect your SEO. Currently, everything that we have covered up to this point has been intended to help you, as a webmaster, achieve two things:

- Ensure your website is indexed properly
- Ensure the content of your website shows properly in the Google Index's search results.

For this to happen correctly, a lot of work from you is required in order to help the search engines do their job properly. Understandably, this seems wrong. The future of SEO (in a year or two) may be a new service illustrated by PubSubHubbub.

The website employs push technology to radically change the way content is published on the Web. Not surprisingly, the PubSubHubbub site and the concept of push have been developed by a Google engineer called Brett Slatkin. Unsurprisingly, again, Google is developing a system that will enable Web publishers of any size to automatically submit new content to Google to be indexed within seconds of that content being published.

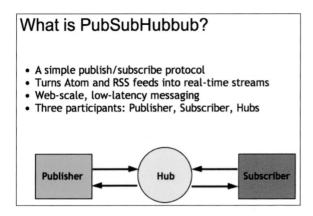

What is PubSubHubbub?

- A simple publish/subscribe protocol
- Turns Atom and RSS feeds into real-time streams
- Web-scale, low-latency messaging
- Three participants: Publisher, Subscriber, Hubs

Potentially this will make publishing a website's content on the Web a lot easier and faster. It will be in the Google Index moments after publication rather than days. For the time being, as a website owner, you need to get involved with *current* real-time Web capabilities. That means you need to have your RSS set up for your website.

Jargon buster

RSS – A technology that is being used by Web users to keep track of their favourite websites. RSS stands for Really Simple Syndication. Many people describe it as a news feed that you subscribe to. When you subscribe to an RSS feed, you tell the RSS reader to let you know every time the website you subscribed to is updated.

RSS is almost universally symbolised by this icon.

10

Setting up an RSS feed to help promote your website

Depending on the kind of website you have, it will most probably come with its own, automatic RSS feed. It will help your SEO immensely, however, if you set up a separate one, also automated using Google's free and very popular Feedburner service ... service.

1. Find your website's RSS feed (usually a URL). If it does not automatically come up with an RSS icon go to your website's homepage right-click and choose **View page source**.

2. When you click on it, you will be able to see (on the next screen) your website's source code. Look for an RSS feed line near the top of the page and make a note of it.

3. Your website's RSS feed is **www.mywebsitename.com/index.php?format=feed& type=rss** and, now that you have this, you are ready for all the next steps.

4. Next, set up your FeedBurner account. Go to **www. feedburner.com** and click **Register** at the top of the page.

5. Fill out the registration form and click **Sign In** once you've done that.

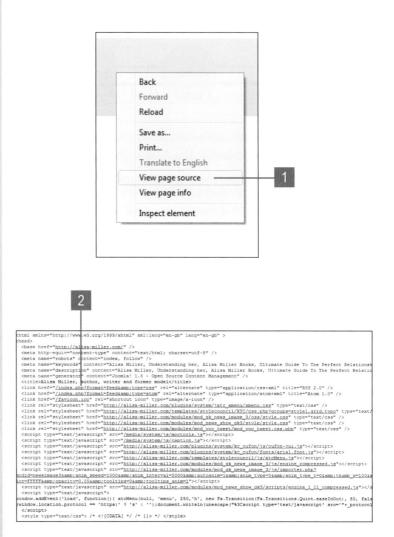

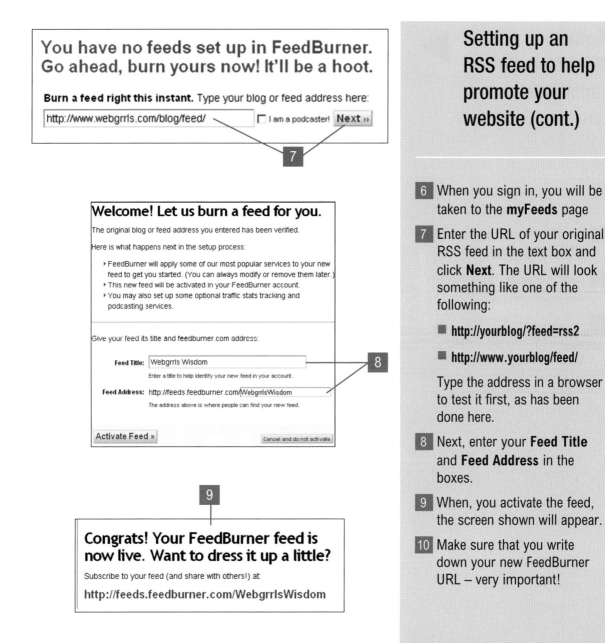

Setting up an RSS feed to help promote your website (cont.)

6 When you sign in, you will be taken to the **myFeeds** page

7 Enter the URL of your original RSS feed in the text box and click **Next**. The URL will look something like one of the following:

- **http://yourblog/?feed=rss2**

- **http://www.yourblog/feed/**

Type the address in a browser to test it first, as has been done here.

8 Next, enter your **Feed Title** and **Feed Address** in the boxes.

9 When, you activate the feed, the screen shown will appear.

10 Make sure that you write down your new FeedBurner URL – very important!

10

Activating FeedBurner's SmartFeed

There are two feed formats – RSS and Atom. Unfortunately, not all feed readers support both formats, so, to ensure compatibility with *all* RSS readers, FeedBurner offers the SmartFeed feature, which will automatically keep track of the feed format each of your subscriber's feed readers supports and display the feed in the correct format.

1. In the manage feed section, click **Optimize** tab.

2. On the services menu on the left, click **SmartFeed**.

3. Click **Activate**. You should see a confirmation.

4. Test your FeedBurner feed address (**http://feeds. feedburner.com/yourFeedName**) in a browser window to make sure that it is working.

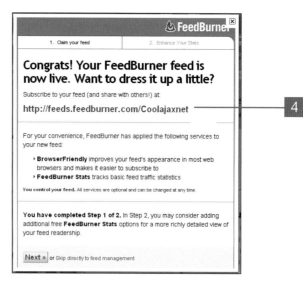

FeedBurner's integration varies depending on which platform you use to publish your blog. Below are links to articles published by Feedburner on how to integrate your Feedburner feed with some of the most popular blog platforms – Blogger, TypePad, Self-Hosted WordPress, WordPress.com and Myspace.

Blogger

- Tracking 100% of your feed traffic: Redirecting your Blogger feed to your FeedBurner feed (at **www.google.com/support/ feedburner/bin/answer.py?answer=78465**)

- How do I promote my FeedBurner feed on my Blogger site? (at: **www.google.com/support/feedburner/bin/answer. py?answer=78467**)

- Adding FeedBurner email to your TypePad or Blogger blog (at: **www.google.com/support/feedburner/bin/answer. py?answer=80874**)

TypePad

- Creating your TypePad's feed **www.google.com/support/ feedburner/bin/answer.py?answer=78478**

- Adding FeedBurner's Publicise features to your TypePad site (at **www.google.com/support/feedburner/bin/answer. py?answer=78480**)

- Adding FeedBurner email to your TypePad or Blogger blog (at: **www.google.com/support/feedburner/bin/answer. py?answer=80874**)

Self-Hosted WordPress

- Creating your WordPress feed (Self-Hosted WordPress) (at: **www.google.com/support/feedburner/bin/answer.py?answer=78483**)

10

Integrating your FeedBurner feed into your blog platform (cont.)

WordPress.com

- Promoting your FeedBurner feed on your WordPress. com site (at: **www.google.com/support/feedburner/bin/answer. py?answer=78487**)

- Offering email subscriptions to your WordPress blog (WordPress.com or Self-Hosted) (at: **www.google.com/ support/feedburner/bin/answer.py?answer=78488**)

Myspace

- Promoting your FeedBurner feed on your Myspace site (at: **www.google.com/support/feedburner/bin/answer.py?answer=78471**)

- Adding FeedBurner email to your Myspace blog (at: **www. google.com/support/feedburner/bin/answer.py?answer=78470**)

Afterword

There is no doubt that the world is changing fast and the Web is changing with it. What used to be exclusively technical and relegated to the more arcane side of website management has now become a vital aspect of online marketing.

If you really want to succeed online, it is no longer enough that you have your website built and fill it with content. You now need to understand what you have to do in order to make it more appealing to search engines and more visible to the human visitors who use search engines to find your website.

There has been a trend over the last five years for SEO and marketing to converge to the point that they are almost indistinguishable. The preceding chapters have taken you through the things you need to do in order to optimise your website correctly, without spending a truckload of money.

Because the Web is changing so fast, it is worth bearing in mind that the techniques and tips given in this book are designed to help you understand all the basics. In SEO there is no practice that goes out of fashion. What usually happens is practices that worked before are watered down as something new comes along, but they are never discarded. That has been the trajectory SEO has taken from the beginning and it has only grown in scope.

By working through this book, you have given yourself a thorough grounding in SEO. You are now ready to face almost anything the online world can throw at you. All you need to do now is put it into effect.

10

Jargon buster

Ad rank – Google AdWords multiplies the quality score (QS) and the maximum cost per click (max CPC) to reach an ad rank score for each ad.

AdSense arbitrage – The process of buying traffic with pay-per-click programs, sending traffic to highly optimised AdSense pages and collecting the difference.

AdSense link-clicking bots – Automated programs that try to spoof random IP addresses to click through AdWords displayed on a site.

Adwords – Google's cost per click (CPC)-based advertising system.

Alt tag – An HTML tag that provides alternative text when non-textual elements – typically images – cannot be displayed.

Alt text – The text that appears when you put the mouse cursor on top of an image or a picture.

Anchor text – Also known as link text or an anchor link – the clickable text of a hyperlink.

API – Application programming interface.

Authority site – A site that has many inbound links coming to it and very few outbound links.

Back link – A text link to your website from another website.

Banned – A term that means a site has been removed from a search engine's index.

Black Hat SEO – A term referring to the practice of 'unethical' SEO. These techniques are used to gain an advantage over your competition.

Blog – A web log that is updated frequently and is usually the opinion of one person. Also, jokingly stands for better listing on Google!

Bot – Short for robot. Often used to refer to a search engine *crawler* or *spider*.

Browser – Software application used to browse the internet. Mozilla Firefox and Internet Explorer are the two most popular browsers.

BTF (below the fold) – This is the part of the user's screen that is hidden unless the user scrolls down on the page.

C class IP – This is the third block of numbers found in an IP Address.

Cache – A copy of Web pages stored within a search engine's database.

CAPTCHA – Stands for completely automated public Turing test to tell computers and humans apart.

Click arbitrage – Purchasing *PPC* ads and hoping that, as traffic leaves, it does so clicking on your ads.

Click distance – The minimum number of clicks it takes a visitor to get from one page to another.

Click flipping – The process of identifying and maximising multiple profit pathways, using PPC traffic and converting that traffic with *CPA* offers.

Click-through – The process of clicking through an online advertisement to the advertiser's destination.

Clickprint – Derived from the amount of time a user spends on a website and the number of pages viewed, a clickprint is a unique online fingerprint that can help a vendor identify return visitors, curb fraud and collect personal information for 'customer service' – aka invasive marketing.

Cloaking – A technique that shows keyword-stuffed pages to a search engine, but a real page to a human user.

Clustering – On search engine search results pages, clustering is limiting each represented website to one or two listings.

Content networks – A nicer way to say link farm – a Black Hat SEO technique and a Google red flag technique.

Content repurposing – A nicer way to say *scraping* a site for content. It will cause your site to be banned.

Contextual link inventory (CLI) – Text links that are shown depending on the content that appears around them.

Conversion optimisation – Transforms your site into a selling tool – your site logically leads visitors through the sales cycle and closes sale.

Conversion rate – The number of visitors to a website who end up performing a specific action that leads to a conversion. This could be a product purchase, signing up to a newsletter sign or anything that involves information being submitted.

Converting search phrase – A phrase that converts traffic into money.

Cookie – Information stored on a user's computer by a website.

Cost per action (CPA) – The price paid for each visitor's actions from a paid search.

Cost-per-click (CPC) – See *Pay-per-click (PPC)*.

CPT (cost per thousand) – The cost for each thousand impressions of your ad.

Crawler – A *bot* from a search engine that reads the text found on a website in order to determine what the website is about.

Cross-linking – Having multiple websites linking to each other.

CSS (cascading style sheets) – Used to define the look and navigation of a website.

CTR (click-through rate) – The value associated with the amount of times a paid ad is viewed.

Dangling link – This term is applied to a Web page with no links to any other pages. Also known as an *orphan page*.

Dead link – A hyperlink pointing to a non-existent URL.

Deep crawl – Once a month, Googlebot will crawl all of the links it has listed in its database on your site. This is known as a deep crawl.

Deep link – A link on a website that is not reachable from the home page.

Delisting – When a site is removed from the search index of a search engine.

Diggbait – Purposely creating content to attract traffic from **digg.com**

Directory – Usually human edited, a directory contains sites that are sorted by categories.

Dmoz – Also known as the open directory project.

DNS (domain name system) – A protocol that lets computers recognise each other through an IP address, whereas humans see websites' URLs.

Doorway page – A Web page designed to draw in Internet traffic from search engines, then direct this traffic to another website.

Dynamic site – A site that uses a database to store its content and is delivered based on the variable passed to the page.

EPC (earnings per click) – How much profit is made from each click from a paid ad.

EPV (earnings per visitor) – The total cost of making profit from a site's total number of visitors.

Error 404 – When a hyperlink is pointing to a location on the Web that doesn't exist, it is called a 404 error.

Everflux – A term associated with the constant updating of Google's algorithm that takes place between the major updates.

External link – A link that points to another website.

FFA (free for all) – A site on which anyone can list their links. Don't waste any time submitting your site to those places.

Filter words – Words such as 'is', 'am', 'were', 'was', 'the', 'for', 'do' and so on, that search engines deem irrelevant for indexing purposes. Also known as stop words.

Flog – A fake blog – that is, a website pretending to be a blog but is actually the creation of a public relations firm, the mainstream media or professional political operatives.

Frames – Frames are an ill-advised way of creating websites so that each page loads other pages in it.

Fresh crawl – When *FreshBot* is used to review already indexed pages and any pages the content of which has been updated.

FreshBot – A sister of GoogleBot's, this *spider* crawls highly ranked sites on a very frequent basis.

Geo targeting – This lets you target your Google ads to specific countries and languages. When you create a new AdWords campaign, you select the countries or regions and the language(s) for your ad. That campaign's ads will appear only to users who live in those areas and who have selected one of those languages as their preference.

GFNR – Google first name rank.

Google AdWords – Google's *PPC* program.

Google bombing – A technique that involves using the same text anchor links to link many people to a certain page, usually of irrelevant content. It has now been largely discounted by subsequent Google algorithm upgrades.

GoogleBot – The *spider* that performs a *deep crawl* of your site.

Googlebowling – To nudge a competitor from the *SERPS*.

Heading tag – Tag that designates headings for the text on a site.

Hidden text – Text that can't be seen normally in a browser.

Hit – A single access request made to the server.

Htaccess – .htaccess is an Apache file that allows server configuration instructions.

HTML (hypertext markup language) – A standardised computer programming language in which Web pages are written.

Hub – A site that has many outbound links and few sites linking back to it.

(inbound Link) – A link residing on another site that points to your site. See also *Outbound link*.

ICRA (Internet Content Rating Association) – The ICRA is an international, non-profit organisation of Internet leaders working to make the Internet safer for children, while respecting the rights of content providers.

Index – A term used to describe the database that holds all the Web pages crawled by the search engine for each website.

Indexing assistance – An even more advanced form of *cloaking*.

Information architecture – The gathering, organising and presenting of information to serve a purpose.

Informational query – When a user makes a query and expects to be provided with information on that topic.

Internal link – A link that points to another page on the same site. Most commonly used for navigation.

Internet traffic optimiser (ITO) – A term for a person who optimises not only for search engines but also to attract traffic from other sources, such as blogs, RSS feeds and articles.

IP address (Internet protocol address) – How data finds its way back and forth from your computer to the Internet.

IP spoofing – A method of reporting an IP address other than your own when connecting to the Internet.

JS (JavaScript) – A scripting language that provides browser functionality.

Keyword density – A ratio of the number of occurrences of a keyword or *keyword phrase* to the total number of words on a page.

Keyword effectiveness index (KEI) – The KEI compares the number of searches for a keyword with the number of search results to pinpoint which keywords should be the most effective for your campaign.

Keyword phrase – A group of words that form a search query.

Keyword stuffing – Using a *keyword* or *keyword phrase* excessively on a Web page, perhaps in the text content or meta tags. This is a banned SEO technique.

Landing page – Usually used in conjunction with a PPC campaign, they are call-to-action pages that prompt users to engage with a site.

Link – Also known as a hyperlink, it is the 'clickable' piece of text or an image that allows for navigation on the Internet.

Link bait (linkbaiting) – The process of getting users to link to your site.

Link farm – A site that features links in no particular order that are totally unrelated to each other. Its main purpose is to provide links rather than content. See also *Content networks*.

Link maximisation – The method of getting popular sites in your industry to link to your website.

Link partner – A website that is willing to put a link to your site on its website. Quite often, link partners engage in reciprocal linking.

Link popularity – How many sites link to your website determines its popularity.

Link text – The clickable part of a hyperlink. Also known as *anchor text* or an anchor link.

Listings – The results that a search engine returns for a particular search term.

Mashups – Commonly thought of as a way of merging two different items or *scraping* more than one source.

Meta description tag – It holds the description of the content found on the page.

Meta keywords tag – It holds the keywords that are found on the page.

Meta search engine – A search engine that relies on the meta data found in *meta tags* to determine relevancy.

Meta tag masking – An old trick that uses CGI codes to hide the *meta tags* from browsers while allowing search engines to actually see the meta tags.

Meta tags – A meta tag is a tag (that is, a coding statement) in the hypertext markup language (*HTML*) that describes some aspect of the contents of a Web page. The information you provide in a meta tag is used by search engines to index a page so that someone searching for the kind of information the page contains will be able to find it.

Meta data – *Meta tags*, or what are officially referred to as meta data elements, are found within the sections of your Web pages.

MFA (made for AdSense) – A term that describes websites created entirely for the purpose of gaming Google AdSense to make money.

MFD – Made for Digg. Similar to *MFA* sites, these sites try to attract traffic from Digg by having entire sites full of funny images or postings.

Mirror sites – A site that exactly duplicates another site.

MSN (Microsoft network) – Microsoft's search engine. Has been relaunched as Bing (allegedly stands for Bing is not Google).

Natural listing – A listing that appears below the sponsored ads, also known as an *organic listings*.

Navigational query – A query that normally has only one satisfactory result.

NOFOLLOW – An attribute used in a hyperlink to instruct search engines to not follow the link (and pass PageRank)

Offpage factors – Factors that alter search engine positions occuring externally from other websites. Having many links from other sites pointing to yours is an example of an offpage factor.

Onpage factors – Factors that determine search engine positions occuring internally within a page on a website. This can include site copy, page titles and the navigational structure of the site. See also *Offpage factors*.

OOP (over optimisation penalty) – A theory that applies if one targets a single *keyword* or *keyword phrase*. The search engines view such linking efforts as *spam*.

Organic listing – The natural results returned by a search engine, also known as a *natural listing*.

Orphan page – A page that has a link to it, but has no links to any other sites.

Outbound link – A link away from your site to any other site.

PageMatch – A *CPC* advertising program that serves your site's ad on a page that contains related content.

PageRank (PR) – An algorithm used by Google to ascribe a numerical value, using a scale from 1 to 10.

Page View – Any time a user looks at any page on a website via his or her browser.

Paid inclusion – A submission service that involves you paying a fee to a search engine in return for that search engine guaranteeing that your website will be included in its index. Paid inclusion programs will also ensure that your website is indexed very fast and *crawled* on regular basis. It can also be used as a term to include a fee-based directory submission.

Pay-for-impressions (PFI) – See *Pay-per-view (PPV)*.

Pay-per-click management – Strategy, planning and placement of targeted keywords in paid search results.

Pay-per-click (PPC) – An Internet marketing formula used to price online advertisements. In PPC programs, the online advertisers will pay the Internet publishers the agreed PPC rate, regardless of whether a sale is made or every time the advert displayed is clicked by a viewer or not. Also called cost-per-click (CPC).

Pay-per-view (PPV) – Another Internet marketing formula used to price online advertisements. In *pay-per-click (PPC)* programs, the online advertisers will pay the Internet publishers the agreed on PPV based on the number of times their advert is displayed. Also called pay-for-impressions (PFI).

PPC – See *Pay-per-click*.

PPV – See *Pay-per-view*.

PR – See *PageRank (PR)*.

Rank or ranking – The actual position of a website on a search engine results page for a certain search term or phrase.

Reciprocal link – When two sites link to each other.

Redirects – Either server-side or scripting language that tells the search engine to go to another URL automatically.

Referral spam – Sending multiple requests to a website, spoofing the header to make it look like real traffic is being sent to another site.

Referrer – The URL of the page that a visitor came from when he or she entered a website.

Relevance rank (RR) – A system in which the search engine tries to determine the theme of a site that a link is coming from.

Relevancy – Term used to describe how close the content of a page is in terms of its relevance to the keyword phrase used in the search box.

Results page – When a user conducts a search, the page that is displayed is called the results page. Sometimes the acronym *SERP* is used, which stands for search engine results page.

Rich Internet applications (RIA) – Applications such as Ajax and Flash that provide a better user experience than the standards applications by delivering content in an on-demand Web environment.

Robot – A term that is often used to refer to a search engine *spider*.

ROC (return on customer) – The value each customer brings to a website.

ROI (return on investment) – The amount that needs to be spent in order to see success on your marketing investment.

RSS (real simple syndication, rich site summary or rich site syndication) – A Web feed format used to publish frequently updated material (such as blog entries, news headlines, audio and videos) in a standardised format that can be read by RSS readers across the Web.

Scraped – When your Web content has been stolen.

Search engine marketing (SEM) – The practice of ensuring that a website is found on the Internet.

Search engine optimisation (SEO) – The act of altering code to a website so that it has optimum relevance for a search engine *spider*.

Search-friendly optimisation (SFO) – As the term implies, this is the process of making a website search engine-friendly.

Search query – The text entered into the search box on a search engine.

SERP (search engine results page) – The results that are displayed after making a query via a search box.

SFO – Search-friendly optimisation.

Sitemap – An XML file that lists all the *URLs* for a website. The XML sitemap file enables a webmaster to inform search engines about URLs on a website that are available for crawling so they are included on the search engine's database. It is, essentially, a roadmap for the content on your website.

Spam – Unwanted e-mails or irrelevant content delivered. Some say it stands for site placed above mine.

Spamming – The act of delivering unwanted messages to the masses.

Spider – The software that *crawls* your site to try and determine the content it finds.

Spiderbaiting – A technique that makes a search engine *spider* find your site.

Splash page – A page displayed for viewing before reaching the main page.

Stickiness – How influential your site is in keeping a visitor on your page.

Strategic linking – A thought out approach to encouraging websites to link to your site.

Submission – The process of submitting URL(s) to search engines or directories.

SWOT – A methodical way of identifying your strengths and weaknesses and examining the opportunities and threats you face.

Theme – What the site's main topic is about.

Title tag – It should be used to describe the Web page using targeted keywords of no more than 60 characters in total, including spaces.

TLD (top-level domain) – Most commonly thought of as a .com, but also includes .org and .edu

Tracking URL – Usually used in *PPC* campaigns, it is a URL that has special code added to it so that results can be monitored.

Traffic – The number of visitors a website receives over a given period. Usually reported on a monthly basis.

Transactional query – A query involving the user expecting to conduct a transaction.

Trusted feed – A form of paid inclusion that uses a bulk XML feed to send website content directly to search engines for indexing. The feed can be optimised so that your website can take advantage of better rankings and, therefore, more traffic.

TrustRank – A method of using a combination of limited human site reviews in conjunction with a search engine algorithm.

Unique visitor – When a user visits a website, his or her IP address is logged so that if he or she returns later on that day, the visit won't be counted as a *unique* visit but as a page impression.

Universal Search – Launched on 16 May 2007, this is Google's attempt to deliver the best results from the Web. It can include videos, images, news, podcasts or any other form of digital content.

URL (uniform resource locator) – The unique address that is used on the Internet in order to identify where a website can be found.

Web saturation – How many pages of your site are indexed by the search engines, collectively.

White Hat SEO – A term that refers to the ethical practice of SEO methodologies adhering to search engines' rules.

Troubleshooting guide